10-7-54

BIG BUSINESS AND THE POLICY

OF

COMPETITION

BIG BUSINESS AND THE POLICY

OF

COMPETITION

BY

CORWIN D. EDWARDS

The Press of Western Reserve University

Cleveland — 1956

1088842

The text of this book is based upon four lectures delivered in Cleveland, Ohio, in April 1955 under the joint sponsorship of Western Reserve University and Case Institute of Technology. The lecture series was made possible by a grant from the Merrill Foundation for Advancement of Financial Knowledge.

TABLE OF CONTENTS

Page

Foreword ix

Chapter I   Issues and Standards in the Appraisal of
              Big Business 1

Chapter II   The Case Against Big Business 27

Chapter III   The Case For Big Business 69

Chapter IV   The Direction of Public Policy 105

Appendix 133

   Table I   Department of Justice Cases 135
   Table II   Federal Trade Commission Cases 157

Index 169

FOREWORD

This volume presents in revised form four lectures delivered in Cleveland in April 1955. They were sponsored jointly by Western Reserve University and Case Institute of Technology under a grant from the Merrill Foundation. Their purpose is to summarize the governmental policy toward big business which, in my opinon, is implied in the anti-trust laws, and state the rationale of that policy. To cover the broad subject with the brevity appropriate to four lectures, it has been necessary to make points baldly, present arguments compactly, and omit many qualifications and elaborations that would be pertinent in a longer statement.

Most of the problems of public policy that arise with reference to big business are generated not by the lively imaginations of public officials or academic observers but by clashes of economic interests, and primarily of business interests. Organized businessmen urge Government to use its power on their behalf or to modify traditional Government policies which they find inconvenient. Other organized businessmen propose conflicting courses of action. Single enterprises request that the Government curb the activity of other enterprises. A Government official cannot long encounter these rival pressures without realizing that businessmen are on all sides of most of the issues confronting him and that few of his decisions can be correctly described as either pro-business or anti-business. Prejudice for or against business as a whole, or any class thereof, is not only improper as a basis for official decision but also typically irrelevant to the issues that arise.

A Government agency can avoid being the plaything of the pressures that are focused upon it only if its objective has been clearly formulated and the relation of its decisions to that objective is clearly understood. There is no substitute for candid discussion in arriving at such a result. It is my hope that these lectures may contribute something to the process.

I should like to express my personal appreciation to the members of the faculty of Western Reserve University and Case Institute of Technology for their many courtesies, and particularly to Sterling McMillan for his critical help in improving the manuscript. However, only I am responsible for whatever error remains.

Corwin D. Edwards

Chicago, Illinois.

CHAPTER I

ISSUES AND STANDARDS IN THE APPRAISAL OF BIG BUSINESS

Political society in the United States is founded upon distrust of concentrated power. We seek to protect our personal freedom by diffusing governmental authority. We do this in three ways: first by spreading the ultimate control over government through-out the entire adult population; second, by limiting the scope of the control which government may exercise over the affairs of the citizens, so that individuals and groups may enjoy the maxi-mum degree of self-determination that we consider feasible; third, by applying a system of checks and balances designed to prevent any one agency of government from abusing or unduly extending its power. We have been frequently told that a more powerful government could do more for us; that a more tightly coordinated government could act more quickly and efficiently; and that a government responsible to the well-informed few rather than to the ignorant many could act more wisely. But these arguments for concentrated political power have not im-pressed us. We, continue to believe that power, being inherently dangerous, should be limited, and that uncurbed power results in abuse of power. Our democratic political tradition still seems to most of us an essential safeguard of vital liberties which we would not lightly abandon.

Competition as a System of Checks and Balances

Belief in competition is the economic corollary of these politi-cal ideas. It, too, rests upon distrust of concentrated power and upon belief in the maximum possible diffusion of rights and opportunities. We are reluctant to see authority over price and production concentrated in one or a few enterprises. We want business rivalries to supply checks and balances that limit the power of each business enterprise. We want all producers and consumers to have a voice in the market decisions that affect them.

Competition, as a political concept, has three aspects. First, it means that each person or organization undertaking to produce and sell or to buy and consume has available a considerable number of alternatives. A worker is not tied to one job; a business man is not tied to one method of production or to one locality or to one group of customers; a buyer is not tied to one source of supply. Each may choose those persons with whom he will deal, and may thus take advantage of the best offers made to him. The larger the number of alternatives available at a given point, and the greater the variety that is to be found in these alternatives, the more fully the situation may be described as competitive.

Second, competition means that vested interests are not protected. A field of business activity is open to new ideas and new organizations, not reserved for established concerns and traditional methods. Of course, existing enterprises inevitably have advantages of experience and reputation; but where competition prevails, the door of opportunity for the new is not closed by legal obstacles nor by boycotts and other forms of organized pressure. Everyone is free to prefer either the new or the old, and the extent of change is determined by the nature of the choices made. This means not only that new undertakings may replace old ones, but also that an established concern is enduringly free to change its way of doing business, to invade new fields of business activity, and to launch new ventures. Freedom to experiment is protected; vested interest is not.

Third, competition means that all persons and organizations engaged in business dealings with one another are basically equal in status and are not hopelessly unequal in bargaining power. None is favored by a preferential position at law nor by avoidable special privilege. None is exposed to ganging-up, that is, to coercion or exploitation growing out of concerted action by others. Though single concerns are likely to differ in size, wealth, and power, there must be some limit, even though an ill-defined one, to the bargaining advantages that grow out of such differences. Exact equality of bargaining strength is not regarded as either feasible or necessary, but great inequality is recognized as a source of weakness in competition.[1] Indeed, differences in bargaining strength may be considered so significant in particular cases as to justify calling the situation monopolistic or oligopolistic rather than competitive.

Thus conceived as the diffusion of economic power, competition is expected to make an important contribution to personal freedom. To consumers it affords an opportunity to ex-

---

[1] In the discussion that follows, the relation between competition and differences in the size and power of business enterprises is central. It must be clear at the outset, however, that the emphasis upon equality in the political philosophy of competition is not as uncompromising as it is in the political philosophy of government. Although we insist upon equality in the political rights and duties of all citizens, we accept as normal the existence of differences in personal wealth. We have become accustomed to differences in business size—first in accepting the idea of a corporation and later in accepting great differences in the size of corporations. Nobody seriously proposes that we try to organize our economic life on the basis of equality as complete as we think is appropriate in the relationship of citizens politically. Nevertheless, we have long been restive and uncertain about the elements of inequality in our economic organization: to make those inequalities palatable we have wanted to believe, first, that they were based upon productive contributions and therefore were both just and functionally necessary, and, second, that they would not develop into such disparities of power as to be inconsistent with competition.

3

press their tastes and preferences in consumption; indeed, the expenditures of consumers are often described as votes determining what shall be produced and who shall produce it. To employees it affords freedom of action and expression on the job, even freedom to speak harshly to the employer, in the knowledge that there are other jobs around the corner. To producers it affords opportunities to choose among various occupations, productive methods, and environments. To each seller and buyer it affords capacity to protect himself by rejecting undesirable transactions for more attractive ones.

Because such elements of self-protection and self-expression are built into the competitive system, there is less need than there would otherwise be for individuals to seek protection by others than themselves. Though individuals, and particularly employed workers, organize private associations for their mutual security, they rely less upon these associations and surrender less of their personal freedom in seeking united strength than would be the case if the protection afforded by competition were not available to them as well. Thus competition keeps the labor union or other private association more consistent with individual liberty than it probably would be in a non-competitive society. Moreover, the opportunity for self-protection limits the need to seek protection from the state through price-fixing, profit limitation, licensing of business enterprises, regulation of the quality of goods, regulation of the treatment of labor, and similar far-reaching controls over the details of business organization and conduct. Consequently there is less risk than in non-competitive societies that the role of government will expand to an extent that jeopardizes political liberty.

Thus competition is valued for its own sake, as the economic equivalent of political democracy, and also as a necessary aid in preserving that democracy by averting dangerous extensions of the power of private organizations and governments.

The political roots of the policy of competition are deeper and older than its economic roots. Indeed, our basic ideas about the danger of concentrated power were developed before the economic theory of competition had attained much currency. It is important to bear this fact in mind; for today the anti-trust laws of the United States are often discussed as though the sole basis for evaluating them were their bearing upon the attainment of strictly economic goals. Undoubtedly the economic impact of the policy of competition must be fully considered. But our interest in abundance of goods and services, full employment of resources, stability, technological progress, and similar economic objectives cannot justify us in disregarding the political foundations of our free society.

Competition as a Source of Good Economic Performance

Competition is traditionally a source of good economic performance as well as human freedom. We have expected competition to force producers to strive for greater efficiency under the incentives of gain if they succeed and bankruptcy if they fail. We have expected it to keep prices low relative to costs, and to reduce both costs and prices as efficiency increases. We have expected it to assure satisfactory quality in the goods we buy. We have expected it to foster experiment as a source of improvement in products and productive processes. We have expected it to generate diversity and variety. We have expected it to check the temptation to restrict output, and thus to promote the maximum use of our productive facilities. We have expected it to provide producers with incomes roughly commensurate with their contributions to the productive process. We have expected it to keep prices, costs, and productive methods flexible, and thus to bring about rapid readjustment to changing conditions. Through this flexibility, we have expected it to give us a suitable balance in the varieties of goods produced and in the proportions of materials and skills used.

In the aggregate such expectations are, of course, Utopian. They have never been fully realized, and today no sophisticated person expects a growing society to attain them fully, either by competition or by any other form of economic organization. Achievement always falls short of aspiration. But after allowing for the imperfections of all human institutions, one must still answer the question whether competition or some other principle will carry us furthest toward our economic goals.

In the last generation faith in the economic results of competition has become considerably more modest than before. We have recognized that competition is not a universal nostrum, and to cope with maladies that it cannot cure we have made exceptions and adopted supplements to the competitive policy. However, there have been two conflicting opinions as to the source of our need for these exceptions. According to one opinion, the competitive principle is incapable of solving all economic problems, no matter how thoroughly it is applied. According to the other opinion, a completely competitive society would produce the desired economic results, but competition can never be fully achieved and therefore economic performance must always be imperfect. Whereas the first opinion approves controls where competition is functionally inappropriate, the second advocates measures to intensify competition at all points, and approves controls to patch the economy where these measures fail.

The dominant opinion of our generation is the former,—that competition, however intense, is not suited to the solution of some of our problems. In accepting this view, we have long recognized that in some fields, such as telephonic communication, technology precludes competition; and in such instances we have accepted monopoly under conditions of public ownership or pervasive public regulation.

6

We have come to recognize that competition does not assure the conservation of scarce resources, and we have superimposed upon our competitive economy various controls for this purpose. We have come to believe that, in fostering lower prices and maximum achievement, competition may press labor too hard and result in work that is too severe, hours that are too long, and wages that are too low. We have adopted labor legislation designed to protect workingmen from such pressure. We have come to think that competition alone does not make the economy sufficiently stable. Accordingly, we have devised various fiscal and financial measures intended to minimize the fluctuations of the business cycle. We have taken it for granted that competition does not automatically result in military preparedness; and we have made substantial departures from the competitive policy in an effort to assure our national strength. We have also set aside competition partially and temporarily in industries where we encountered special emergencies; and we have allowed some of these temporary measures, such as our agricultural price supports, to develop into enduring exceptions to the general rule of competition. In the aggregate our programs of control constitute substantial supplements or substitutes for competition and reflect a substantial weakening of our belief that competition necessarily assures good economic performance.

Nevertheless, our departures from the competitive principle have been reluctant and limited in scope. We have continued to regard competition as the norm. Where we have set competition aside we have usually tried to make the exception as narrow as possible. Moreover, we have placed the burden of proof upon those who advocate an exception. They are expected to show that competition cannot accomplish an important public purpose and that a substitute for competition can do so. They are expected to include in their substitute program such safeguards of the public interest as are needed to constitute a rough

7

equivalent for the competition that is set aside. They are expected to obtain specific governmental approval for the program.

These requirements have meant that the state may reduce the scope of competition, but private persons may not do so. Most instances in which we have made exceptions to the competitive regime have provided, not a broader field for uncontrolled monopoly, but an extension of state control. In the few cases where this is probably not so,—for example, the resale price maintenance legislation—the facts are in dispute, and competition probably would not have been abandoned if the situation replacing it had been recognized as one of uncurbed private power. In losing parts of our faith in competition, we have not acquired a new faith in private monopoly. We still believe that monopoly is characterized by high prices, restricted output, unstable production and employment, repressive labor policies, and waste of resources. If competition alone does not solve the problems of conservation, labor standards, stability, and preparedness, private monopoly, we believe, would do so even less. We think that competition contributes something toward the mitigation of these problems.[1] We conceive the necessary supplementary measures as public action rather than non-competitive private action. We have continued to look with distrust upon private concentrations of power, and have continued to assume that such concentrations not only are politically dangerous but also have bad economic effects.

Hence we have regarded the political and economic aspects of our competitive policy as generally harmonious. We have defended competition with political or economic arguments

---

[1] The Employment Act of 1946 declares it to be the function of the Council of Economic Advisers to recommend to the President "national economic policies to foster and promote free competitive enterprise, to avoid economic fluctuations or to diminish the effects thereof, and to maintain employment, production, and purchasing power." 60 *Stat.* 25.

as was most convenient, but have tended to give primacy to the political ones. The Report of the Attorney General's National Committee to Study the Antitrust Laws, issued in March 1955, begins with a unanimous declaration by nearly 60 lawyers and economists, who constituted the committee, that "Antitrust is a distinctive American means for assuring the competitive economy on which our political and social freedom under representative government in part depend. These laws have helped release energies essential to our leadership in industrial production and technological development. They reinforce our ideal of careers open to superior skills and talent, a crucial index of a free society. As a result, the essentials of anti-trust are today proclaimed by both political parties as necessary to assure economic opportunity and some limitation on economic power incompatible with the maintenance of competitive conditions."[1] Similarly, in deciding the antitrust case against the Aluminum Company of America in 1945, Judge Learned Hand said:[2]

---

[1] *Report,* Government Printing Office, 1955, p. 2.

[2] 148 Fed. 2d., 427-429. A similar view was expressed by Justice Douglas in the Columbia Steel Case, but since it appears in a dissenting opinion it lacks authority as an interpretation of the law. "In final analysis, size in steel is the measure of the power of a handful of men over our economy. That power can be utilized with lightning speed. It can be benign or it can be dangerous. The philosophy of the Sherman Act is that it should not exist. For all power tends to develop into a government in itself. Power that controls the economy should be in the hands of elected representatives of the people, not in the hands of an industrial oligarchy. Industrial power should be decentralized. It should be scattered into many hands so that the fortunes of the people will not be dependent on the whim or caprice, the political prejudices, the emotional stability of a few self-appointed men. The fact that they are not vicious men but respectable and social-minded is irrelevant. That is the philosophy and the command of the Sherman Act. It is founded on a theory of hostility to the concentration in private hands of power so great that only a government of the people should have it." *U. S. v Columbia Steel Co.,* 334 U.S. 536.

"It is possible, because of its indirect social or moral effect, to prefer a system of small producers, each dependent upon his own skill and character, to one in which the great mass of those engaged must accept the direction of a few . . . We have been speaking only of the economic reasons which forbid monopoly; but, as we have already implied, there are others, based upon the belief that great industrial consolidations are inherently undesirable, regardless of their economic results. In the debates in Congress Senator Sherman himself . . . showed that among the purposes of Congress in 1890 was a desire to put an end to great aggregations of capital because of the helplessness of the individual before them. . . . Throughout the history of these statutes it has been constantly assumed that one of their purposes was to perpetuate and preserve, for its own sake and in spite of possible cost, an organization of industry in small units which can effectively compete with each other."

Inconsistencies Between Big Business and Competition

The problem of big business has arisen in the perspective provided by our belief in the diffusion of political and economic power. Traditionally we have doubted that an economy of large business units can be a competitive economy. There is an obvious structural inconsistency between the pattern appropriate to competition and the pattern of big business. Within any given industry or market, the number of enterprises necessarily becomes smaller as the average size of these concerns becomes larger. A market in which all sellers or buyers are big is one in which they are few. If they are big enough, they may be so few that few alternatives are available to persons who deal with them. Thus the opportunity for competitive self-protection by their customers or suppliers may be impaired.

Where big companies have small competitors, small suppliers, or small customers, there may be a substantial inequality of bargaining power between the big and those who must deal with them or compete with them. Whether or not the large concern has an advantage over the small in productive techniques and operating costs, it is likely to be able to outwait its small customer or supplier, to outbid its small rival, and to diversify its source of income so that it is not dependent, like the small enterprises, upon the fortunes of one market. So far as differentials in size result in such differences in the capacity to compete and to survive, they may further enhance the bigness of the big and may also induce undue docility among the small. They may weaken the effectiveness of the checks and balances of competition.

Where there are big companies, the opportunity for new business ventures may be substantially weakened. The scale of production may require so much capital that few newcomers can furnish it. The prestige and connections of well-established large enterprises may constitute barriers to new competition that can be overcome only slowly and at great expense. The opportunities for newcomers may be reduced by the pervasive forethought of the big companies in acquiring large reserves of raw materials, in making long term contracts with important customers and suppliers, and in devolping vertical integration which channels the flow of much of the product among affiliated establishments. As entry into business, or into a new field of business, becomes more difficult, the range of experiment may be reduced and the position of vested interests may become stronger.

The diversification of the big company may also diminish responsiveness to market forces, as reflected in prices and profits. Many of the activities of a large enterprise have no great influence upon its total profits, and may be readily supported from the profits of other activities. The influences of vested interests and established policies is against change, and the diffused attention of management may tend to reduce awareness of the considerations that call for change. Thus there is in bigness a tendency to substitute administrative planning for competitive response.

Finally, if business enterprises are few, as they must be if they are large, and if they are in constant contact with one another, as they are likely to be, they may easily agree to set aside competition among themselves. Bigness makes possible the gentlemen's agreement among a few like-minded associates, possibly developed on the golf course or at the luncheon table. Indeed, economic theorists have emphasized the point that, where competitors are very few, each concern may be able to develop its own policies with confidence that it can predict what its rivals will do in consequence; and such a mutual reading of minds is said to produce concerted action that cannot be distinguished from the results of a formal agreement. Though the ease and frequency of such mind-reading has been grossly exaggerated in theoretical writing, it is significant that such a relationship only becomes plausible when rivals are large and few.

In summary, then, big business may be inconsistent with the competitive policy in that it unduly reduces the variety of alternatives available to traders on the other side of the market; impairs the independence and success of small traders through differences in power derived from differences in size; places significant obstacles in the way of new competitors; diminishes the responsiveness of large concerns to the pecuniary incentives of particular markets; and facilitates the development of concerted policies in the place of policies independently determined.

But this structural inconsistency between the patterns of bigness and competition can be easily over-emphasized. Each of the discrepancies may exist in varying degrees. While it is obvious that extreme concentration of economic power would destroy competition, it is also obvious that the competitive policy does not require complete uniformity in the size and power of economic units. In many markets some concerns can be relatively big without such a reduction in number as precludes variety. There can be differences in size that have no crucial effect upon bargaining power or upon the opportunity to start new enterprises. Some degree of diversification can be consistent with responsiveness to market forces. Concerted action is not inevitable even when business rivals are relatively few. Though anti-competitive results may appear if bigness is pushed too far, lesser degrees of bigness may not even make them probable. The important and disputed question concerns the degree of concentration at which significant dangers may be expected to arise.

Is Big Business Getting Bigger?

There is a widespread belief that industrial concentration in the United States is already dangerously high and is still growing. In 1932 Berle and Means predicted[1] that if the relative rate of growth of big companies which had prevailed from 1909 to 1929 were continued, by 1950 70 percent of all corporate activity would be carried on by 200 corporations. This forecast was not even approximately correct. Recent studies of concentration indicate that there has not been any great change in the last two decades. The most significant computations are those for manufacture and distribution, areas in which we rely upon competition with the least admixture of public control. The Federal Trade Commission has reported that the top 200 manufacturing corporations shipped 37.7 percent of the shipments of all manufacturing enterprises in 1935 and that their share had grown by not quite 3 percentage points to 40.5 percent in 1950.[2]

[1] Adolph A. Berle, and Gardiner Means, *The Modern Corporation and Private Property*, (New York, Macmillan Company) p. 40.

[2] Federal Trade Commission, *Report on Changes in Concentration in Manufacturing, 1935 to 1947 and 1950*, (Washington D. C. U.S. Government Printing Office, 1954) p. 17.

A.D.H. Kaplan of the Brookings Institution has estimated[1] that in 1929 the 100 largest industrial corporations had 25.5 percent of the assets, and 43.4 percent of the income before taxes, of all industrial corporations. According to his estimates, by 1948 the corresponding percentage of assets was 26.7, a rise of 1.2 percentage points, and the corresponding percentage of profits was 30.4, a fall of 13 percentage points. Relying upon different sets of figures and different years for comparison, economists have disputed whether the recent trend of concentration is upward or downward. There is general agreement, however, that the change since 1929 in the percentage of business done by the largest industrial corporations has not been great.

Since the largest industrial companies have grown at a rate roughly equal to the rate of growth of industrial activity generally, they are obviously not taking over the industrial field at the catastrophic pace predicted by Berle and Means. We are no longer faced with the necessity of solving the concentration problem in a few years unless events are to take the decision out of our hands. Thus it is possible to discuss the matter with less sense of urgency than during the 1930's. However, if concentration has not greatly increased in the last two or three decades, it has also not significantly diminished. Whatever problems it raised in 1929 are still with us; and nothing we know about the trend of corporate size can support the optimistic belief that the growth of the economy will automatically reduce the relative power of our large enterprises. Instead, since the biggest companies have grown with the economy, they are bigger than before, and it is therefore probable that their size relative to the smallest companies has increased. We have been given an extension of time, but have not been relieved of the necessity of exam-

---

[1] A. D. H. Kaplan, *Big Enterprise in a Competitive System*, (Washington, D. C., Brookings Institution, 1954) pp. 126-127.

ining the problems raised by big business and determining what we should do about them.

Recent Defenses of Big Business

In evaluating concentration, we must now take account of a new phenomenon, the vigorous defense of big business by persons who cannot be disregarded as mere propagandists for vested interests. Theorists formulate, sooner or later, a rationale for every important power group; and these theories, adopted by the power groups to explain and defend their activities, become important weapons in the clash of ideas that usually accompanies a conflict of interests. Where there is such a clash of ideas, social adjustment is partly the result of argument. In an atmosphere of argument, extreme views are usually eliminated, and there is likely to be compromise on non-essentials. Thus conflict of theories reduces the role of sheer economic and political force in a struggle between power groups. Such idealogical rivalry should be welcomed, and the lack of a suitable rationale by any important power group should be regarded, not only as a weakness in that group's position, but also as a handicap to the development of a satisfactory adjustment of social conflicts.

The theories of competition have provided a ready-made rationale for the critics of big business, but until recently big business has had no equivalent defensive rationale. Such a gap cannot be filled by bursts of propaganda. It requires dispassionate analysis by theorists who believe they have found an aspect of the truth and who have no personal ends to serve. In the last few years several versions of a rationale of big business have been formulated. They differ in many respects; but they all agree in asserting that there is no need for us to cling to our traditional distrust of concentrated business power.

Five different lines of argument have been used to reach this conclusion. The first has been offered by several writers, and notably by the National Association of Manufacturers. According to this argument, the beneficience of big business is attested by the obvious successes of the American economic system. Our standards of living, already high, are rising rapidly because of rising productivity and technical progress. We have little unemployment of men or resources. Goods that elsewhere are luxuries are produced here for a mass market and sold at prices that will move them into consumption by people whose wages are high enough to buy them. Such results are expected to flow from competition, not from monopoly. Hence one may persuasively infer that our economy is actually competitive.[1] Since the tone of the economy is determined by big business, big business, too, must be basically competitive.

Closely related to this argument is a second one, formulated by Joseph Schumpeter,[2] who until his death was professor of economics at Harvard. As he sees the large business enterprise, it is engaged in a process of creative destruction that is essentially competitive. It explores technological frontiers and emerges with new products and processes. Such innovations are likely to set new standards of quality, costs, and prices, to destroy established ways

---

[1] "The result of effective competition is growth and progress, with a continual increase in the output of goods at continually lower prices. The result of monopoly power is the reverse: prices are maintained by curtailing volume and economic growth is stunted. By this overall criterion there can be no doubt that the United States has enjoyed the advantages of aggressive competition. The growth of the economy, the constant appearance of new products, the increase in output of goods, and the constant improvement of the standard of living, are all evidence of this fact. Whatever may happen in the future, there is as yet no sign that business concentration, by destroying competition, has brought our economic progress to an end." Taken from National Association of Manufacturers, *Business Size and the Public Interest,* (Economic Policy Division Series No. 18, November, 1949, Summary, paragraph 12.)

[2] Joseph Schumpeter, *Capitalism, Socialism and Democracy,* (New York, Harper & Brothers, 1942.)

of doing things, and to force concerns committed to the old ways to change or die. The competitive pressure thus developed constitutes a super-competition more substantial and significant than the ordinary rivalry among concerns that produce the same thing in the same way. It is at once destructive competition and the essence of creative progress. Schumpeter draws the conclusion that so long as this creative destruction takes place we need not worry about preserving more conventional forms of competition. Indeed, he thinks we need not feel concern over most monopolistic restrictions, which, in his interpretation, are usually efforts to provide such temporary stability as is needed for technological pioneering.

A third line of argument, formulated, by A. D. H. Kaplan of the Brookings Institution,[1] also reaches the conclusion that big business is essentially competitive, but by a different route. To Kaplan the large enterprise has a long-run perspective which induces it to behave competitively. Most forms of monopolistic advantage are ephemeral, and to exploit them is to sacrifice opportunities for long-run growth. Moreover, the desire of each large enterprise to grow brings it into an inevitable conflict with other large companies that have similar desires. Again, the large concern has within it a considerable number of subordinate executives, each ambitious to achieve something startling and thereby enhance his personal success. In Kaplan's opinion a restrictively-minded top executive would have great difficulty in repressing these ambitions.

According to a fourth line of argument, also formulated by Kaplan,[2] we need not fear the big companies because their power is precarious and unstable. At any one moment, the largest make an impressive show of dominance, but from decade to decade

---

[1] A. D. H. Kaplan, *Big Enterprise in a Competitive System, op. cit.,* especially Chapter 9.
[2] *Ibid,* Chapter 7.

many of the old concerns are replaced at the top of the industrial pyramid by new ones. Most of them are not strong enough to hold their relative positions; and the rise of the new concerns is evidence of the dynamically competitive relationships that prevail.

A fifth line of argument, developed by Kenneth Galbraith,[1] also a professor at Harvard, relies upon the protection afforded by countervailing power. Unlike Kaplan and Schumpeter, Galbraith believes that big companies accumulate substantial power and would use it objectionably if not curbed. However, he sees protection for the public in the fact that power accumulates at many points. Big seller faces big buyer; big employer faces big union; big company faces big government. The scale of social conflict and of social control is changing, but the larger aggregates offset each other, and the result is not the restriction and exploitation that would be produced by disparities of power, but something approaching a system of equitable bargains.

Though partially complementary to one other, these five types of argument[2] are contradictory in various respects. Schum-

---

[1] Galbraith, John Kenneth, *American Capitalism, The Concept of Countervailing Power,* (Boston, Houghton-Mifflin Co., 1952). A somewhat similar view is expressed by David Lilienthal, former head of the Tennesee Valley Authority, in *Big Business, A New Era* (New York, Harper & Brothers, 1953). To him the expansion in the role of government in economic affairs after 1933, reinforced by the new power of organized labor and the increased power of large buyers, has reduced the danger of big business to manageable proportions. However, Mr. Lilienthal's views also resemble those of Mr. Kaplan in that he does not think the danger very great in any event. He stresses an increase in the social responsibility of big business, and asserts that "Our productive and distributive superiority, our economic fruitfulness, rest upon Bigness. Size is our greatest single functional asset." (p.33)

[2] A sixth favorable view of big business, expressed by A. A. Berle, Jr., *The Twentieth Century Capitalist Revolution,* (New York, Harcourt, Brace & Co., 1954) has been disregarded in this summary, primarily because it is concerned with a time span, and rests upon appraisals, that

peter admits the frequent existence of monopolistic restrictions by large companies, but sees them as necessary, though unimportant, details in a competitive picture. Kaplan regards restrictions as inconsistent with the basic purposes and policies of large enterprises and as usually impossible because of the competitive struggle between such concerns. Galbraith thinks that the purposes of big companies may be basically restrictive, but that these purposes are thwarted by the strength of the potential victims. Schumpeter thinks the power of big companies is adequately checked by the competition of other big companies. Kaplan thinks the curb is applied not only by large competitors but also by small ones. Galbraith places his confidence, not in the com-

---

fall outside the scope of this book. To Mr. Berle concentrated corporate power, associated with great productivity and relatively unchecked by the investment market or by competition, is the central fact of our economic organization. He thinks this power is now partially curbed by public opinion, the political authority of the state, and the rivalry of oligopolists for leadership. He thinks it will gradually develop institutions expressing the corporate conscience, as royal power developed equity procedures to express the king's conscience. But his attention is upon the slow evolution of political institutions, not upon today's unsolved problems of corporate power. Moreover, he is concerned with political order and the planning relevant thereto rather than with the economic quality of the result attained. Thus he praises the world-wide system of marketing quotas developed in the petroleum industry under the Achnacarry agreement as "the most successful experiment in economic world government thus far achieved in the twentieth century," (p. 147) on the ground that "there was peace, and there was production, and there was distribution, and there was a stable and reasonably acceptable price." (p. 155). Recognizing the possibility that under the agreement profits were too high, prices were greater than necessary, and group operations tended to discourage local development of crude supply and refining capacity, he dismisses such criticisms with the comment that "in any planned economy, national or international, production and stability is gained at the expense of some restriction of freedom of action" (p. 156). Thus he rejects both the political and the economic preconceptions which are starting points for this book.

petitive power of business rivals, but in the offsetting power of suppliers and customers. In spite of these disagreements as to how much power big business enjoys, what checks upon that power are effective, and how far that power would be used restrictively if unchecked, all three draw the same conclusion, that big business as it now functions can be regarded, not as a source of dangers that demand precaution, but as a beneficent force, adequately controlled by its own purposes, its economic environment, or both together.

It is noteworthy that these attempts at a rationale of big business are incomplete. Of the five lines of argument, four are addressed primarily to the question of economic performance, with little or no attention to questions of freedom and opportunity in economic life. Schumpeter sees no political problem in his conclusion that economic progress is primarily a function of the large enterprise. Finding that small concerns continue to be numerous and that the biggest companies are not securely perched at the pinnacle of size, Kaplan apparently feels no need to discuss the impact of bigness upon the community except in economic terms. Only Galbraith deals explicitly with political espects of economic power, and even he is content with a sort of mutual stalemate among would-be economic despots. In general, the instabilities and rivalries among powerful enterprises, and the enlightened self-interest which these enterprises show, are conceived as adequate protection for the community in the political aspects of economic life. This view is scarcely more persuasive than would be a contention that the liberties of citizens and the rights of small nations are adequately safeguarded by the instabilities and rivalries of national governments.

It is also noteworthy that these defenses of big business point toward a general evaluation rather than toward a formula for appraising particular large enterprises. Our policy of competition rests primarily upon the anti-trust laws, which are enforced by a series of cases against designated enterprises, not by general evaluations. Under these laws the entire body of big enterprises cannot be attacked. An anti-trust case involving bigness is directed against one or more large companies and is based upon the charge that these particular companies have impaired competition or are in process of doing so. A general evaluation of big business is irrelevant to such a case. No matter how competitive big business may be generally, the defendants in the particular case must be condemned if they have set aside competition. No matter how monopolistic big business may be generally, the particular defendants must not be condemned if they have done nothing to jeopardize competition. In enforcing the anti-trust laws one needs criteria by which the competitiveness of a particular enterprise can be determined in a particular setting. One is not helped by opinions that big business, or any other class of business, is generally good or generally bad.

It is true, of course, that in various anti-trust cases the size of the defendant company has been considered relevant to that company's guilt or innocence. Percentage of the market has long been regarded as one element of proof that there is an actual or potential monopoly. In some recent cases the size of the big company relative to suppliers, customers, or rivals appears to have carried weight in justifying an inference of monopoly where the percentage of the market is lower than that customarily thought to be monopolistic.[1] In other recent cases behavior which would not be questioned on the part of a small concern has been interpreted as having a monopolistic purpose or effect when engaged in by a big company. Thus vertical integration by a large company has been interpreted as monopolistic pre-emption of a portion of the supply of raw materials or a portion of the market for

---

[1] *U.S. v. E. I. duPont de Nemours, complaint, June 30, 1949.* The lower court acquitted and the Government's appeal is now pending.

finished products,[1] on the theory that so much of the total has been acquired that independant concerns deprived of this portion of the market must suffer. In one case refusal by a single large company to deal with particular suppliers was interpreted as the equivalent of an illegal boycott, even though smaller enterprises may freely decide with whom they will trade.[3] Where the government has questioned long-term contracts for the sale of goods,[2] or exclusive dealing arrangements,[3] or arrangements by which machines are leased rather than sold to their users,[4] these arrangements have been thought to be inconsistent with competition partly because of the bigness of the companies initiating them. Most striking of all, receipt of a substantial discount by a large distributor upon a commodity bought for resale has been interpreted by the Supreme Court as inherently injurious to competition and hence as unlawful under the Robinson-Patman Act.[5] The anti-trust laws condemn, not bigness, but restraints of trade and tendencies toward monopoly. Nevertheless, since the impact of a business practice varies with the size of the concerns that engage in it, types of action that are permissible for business generally may be condemned as monopolistic in tendency when undertaken by big business.

But though such judgments turn upon questions of size, they do not rest upon a broad evaluation of bigness generally. In each instance an issue is raised whether a specific degree and kind of bigness, when related to a specific set of practices, tends to destroy competition in a specific setting. The issue is determ-

---

[1] *U.S. v. New York Great Atlantic & Pafific Tea Co., op. cit.*

[2] *U.S. v. American Can Co.,* 87 Fed. Supp. 18.

[3] *U.S. v. Standard Oil Co. of California and Standard Stations, Inc.* 78 Fed. Supp. 850, 337 U.S. 293.

[4] *U.S. v. American Can Co., op.cit. U.S. v. United Shoe Machinery Co.,* 110 Fed. Supp. 295.

[5] *Morton Salt Co. v. Federal Trade Commission,* 334 U.S. 37.

ined by specific evidence and inference from it, not by a philosophy as to the general desirability of bigness. The only broad opinion which is necessary to the handling of such cases is one that no sympathizer with big business would dispute—namely, that under some circumstances some degrees of bigness are capable of reinforcing some monopolistic tendencies.

This comment is not meant to imply, however, that the efforts to formulate a rationale for big business have been irrelevant to the policy of competition. The point is merely that the arguments thus far developed are not relevant to the anti-trust laws as a major expression of that policy and do not provide ideas which, if accepted, might contribute to a more discriminating enforcement of those laws.

Nevertheless, the general appraisal of big business probably has a practical effect upon the vigor with which the anti-trust laws are applied to large companies. Belief that the impairment of competition by big business is infrequent and unimportant does not encourage frequent scrutiny of large enterprises or suspicious investigation of conduct by such enterprises that might be interpreted as restrictive or monopolistic. Belief, such as Schumpeter's, that monopolistic restrictions are minor incidents of overriding policies that provide good economic performance encourages inaction when such restrictions are encountered and might lead to amendment of law and policy to substitute for the competitive principle some other principle based directly upon economic performance. Conversely, belief that big business characteristically reduces competition and thus jeopardizes both political freedom and economic performance is likely to result in constant surveillance of large enterprises and prompt action wherever evidence of anti-competitive effects actually appears. Though the broad appraisal of big business has no logical relation to the anti-trust policy, it has an important psychological one.

Apart from anti-trust policy, there have been laws and proposals intended to curb big business as such or to foster small business as such. Belief that big busines is generally dangerous and that small business is jeopardized unless given public support has been the stimulus to such measures.

The most striking example of such a program is the chain-store tax legislation enacted by many states during the 1930's. In such laws a tax levied upon retail establishments becomes progressively greater with each increase in the number of establishments under a common ownership. The avowed purpose of the legislation was to limit the size of retail chain stores. Although few other governmental measures have been equally explicit, several have been affected by the climate of opinion as to big business. Federal legislation has established in recent years a succession of agencies especially devoted to the interests of small business, with such functions as lending money to small concerns under conditions and upon terms not commercially attractive and assuring the award of some proportion of government contracts to small concerns in spite of the availability of bids by larger suppliers offering more attractive terms. From time to time competition has been limited by statutes such as the state laws forbidding sales below cost or authorizing sellers of branded goods to fix resale prices and enforce compliance therewith; and the principal argument for such legislation has been that it would protect small business from large business.

Moreover, there have been suggestions for legislation to limit the bigness of big companies generally. So far as I know, no official of a Federal agency has formally endorsed any such plan. But the idea has had responsible private endorsement. In 1950 Senator Robert Taft suggested that Congress "should consider whether we should place a limit on the proportion of any industry which can be controlled by one company."[1] In 1951 a Com-

---

[1] Quoted in David E. Lilienthal, *Big Business, A New Era,* (New York, Harper & Brothers, 1953) pp. 136-137.

mittee of the Twentieth Century Fund recommended that concerns which attain a given level of bigness be required to prove that further expansion would be useful to the public before being allowed to undertake it.[1]

In considering laws and proposals such as these, a general evaluation of big business is relevant. The appropriate issue for such an evaluation is whether the effects of big business are so generally good or bad that policy should be based upon a comprehensive judgment, or, alternatively, so mixed and various that public policy should rely upon the case-by-case procedure of our anti-trust laws.

Summary

To summarize: The policy of competition is deeply rooted in the political traditions of American democracy and also well rooted in the belief that a competitive economy is necessary to give us good economic performance. Though the latter belief has been modified somewhat by acceptance of the need for governmental controls for various purposes, with respect to uncontrolled private monopoly both beliefs are still vigorous. In several ways the pattern of big business appears to be inconsistent with the competitive pattern, and, partly for this reason, big business is suspected of impairing competition. Recently, however, five kinds of rationale for big business have been formulated, which, though different in important respects, have in common the assertion that the anti-competitive aspects of big business are non-existent or unimportant. Though a broad evaluation of big

---

[1] George Stocking, & Myron Watkins, *Monopoly and Free Enterprise,* (New York, Twentieth Century Fund, 1951). This volume contains a report by the Twentieth Century Fund's Committee on Cartels and Monopoly, which at pp. 563-564, includes the recommendation (from which one member of the Committee dissented).

business is not relevant to the public policy of the anti-trust laws. which proceeds case by case and presumes that cases will differ, it probably affects the zeal with which those laws are enforced. It is also relevant to other possible types of public policy in which big business generally would be encouraged or curbed because of implications derived from its size; and there are some laws and legislative proposals which reflect this latter conception of policy.

CHAPTER II

THE CASE AGAINST BIG BUSINESS

To provide a foundation for discussion of public policy, it is necessary to consider the degree of truth that lies in the claims that are made for and against big business. This chapter discusses the extent of the power of large enterprises and the evidence that this power is used to the detriment of the public—the case against big business. The following chapter considers the evidence as to the competitive forces bearing upon big business and the achievements of big business in the public interest—the case for big business. The final chapter is concerned with the implications of both types of evidence for public policy.

The democratic principle is that, since highly concentrated power involves grave risk of abuse, power should be highly concentrated only so far as is necessary to serve some public purpose. A political evaluation of big business turns, therefore, on two questions: First, how powerful are large companies? and second, is their power functionally useful to the public? Power that has no functional usefulness should be eliminated not only when it is actually abused but also where it is so great as to create substantial danger of abuse.

Power Aspects of Big Business

Power is not easily measured. It is attained in many ways, some of which are subtle, and the semblance of power does not always coincide with the possession of it. He who has a position in which power appears to be inherent may be curbed in practice by his environment or by his own ineptitude. He who exercises control over others may do so overtly and indeed conspicuously so long as his uncertain authority might be successfully challenged, but may limit himself to suggestion when his power has become so great that his wish is equivalent to a command. Thus neither the position nor the behavior of an enterprise can be an infallible indicator of its power. Neither can a concern's impressions of its own power nor the impressions of those who deal with the concern; for power often is thought to be limited by those who exercise it and unlimited by those who are subject to it. Whatever evidence may be regarded as indicative of the power of a business enterprise, many subtle influences tending to enhance or reduce that power will necessarily be overlooked.

Nevertheless, men in society have always recognized that there is meaning in distinctions between equal and unequal power, between small and large disparities of power, between the powerful and the weak. The concept of power is slippery, but we use it because we have no better way of coming to grips with one part of political reality.

The distinctive power of big business is derived from its bigness. Obviously business enterprises may obtain power from many other sources—political privilege, franchises and patents, established reputation, efficient management, or a favorable market environment. If these sources of power are peculiarly available to the big, they reenforce and may be regarded as supplements to the power derived from bigness. If they are peculiarly available to small companies, they offset bigness as a source of power and mitigate its effects. But except when these other advantages are associated with bigness or are inconsistent with bigness, they must be presumed to fall indiscriminately upon the big and the little and thus are irrelevant to a discussion of business size. The significant question here is the degree of power that is to be attributed directly or indirectly to bigness itself.[1]

Monopoly Power

The power of large enterprises has several aspects. The one which is most familiar is monopoly.[2] A monopoly may be defined as a concern which does so much of the business of a market or industry that it effectively controls the whole of that business. Under any given set of circumstances, the likelihood that monopoly has been attained grows with each increase in the percentage of the market under a single control. Hence percentage of the market is widely regarded as a rough measure of monopoly power. Where the market is large, a concern can have a large percentage of it only if the concern is also large.

In practice, a stated high percentage of the market may repre-

---

[1]The National Association of Manufacturers has failed to recognize this point. Its pamphlet, *Business Size and the Public Interest,* declares (Summary, paragraph 11) that "The size, and the number, of independent companies operating in any field is one, but only one, of the factors which determine the character of competition in that field. Other factors are equally important in determining the vigor of the competitive struggle: the nature of the product (whether it is standardized or unstandardized), the method of quoting prices, the alertness of buyers and their fund of information about the market, and many other factors, have a bearing on the state of competition." The other factors listed are not said to have any effect in reducing or offsetting the impact of the size and number of business enterprises. They are merely mentioned as independent variables. So far as they have no characteristic relation to the size or number of companies, they do not, of course, offset or accentuate whatever effects spring from size and number. If the effect of size or number is significant, policies appropriate to that effect need not wait because other conditions have effects also.

[2]Buyers, as well as sellers, may have power. Monopsony is the buyer's equivalent of monopoly. For simplicity's sake, the discussion that follows will ignore monopsony power except where it is unlike monopoly power.

sent widely different degrees of power in different industries. The degree of power differs with the intensity of the buyers' need, since the monopolist can exercise less control over customers who would readily forego the product than over customers who think they must have it. The degree of power also differs with the degree of isolation that prevails for the controlled market. If substitute commodities are not available from other companies, if producers in other markets cannot readily ship into the controlled one, and if new concerns cannot readily get started, the monopolist may enjoy great power. Conversely, if substitutes are plentiful and good, if shipment from outside is easy, and if entry into business is easy, there may be an appearance of monopoly without actual monopoly power. The degree of monoply power also differs with the nature of the remaining competitors—— whether the remainder of the market is supplied by one concern or many, whether these additional suppliers are dependent upon one market or have strength derived from various industries, and whether their portion of the supply can be readily expanded.

When such variables are considered, it is evident that in many cases a small enterprise may produce a large percentage of a relatively unimportant product, sold to a limited market, without possessing much monopoly power. Where (a) capital requirements are low, (b) no large marketing organization is needed, and (c) the technology is simple enough to be easily learned, concerns not now engaged in the business may enter it readily unless they are blocked by patents or other legal obstacles. Under such circumstancs, even if no substitutes are available, the small company's dominance is likely to depend upon setting prices low enough and keeping quality high enough to make the market relatively unattractive to outsiders or upon keeping the whole undertaking small enough that outsiders do not bother to investigate its possibilities.

The monopoly that is likely to have significant power (when

30

not protected by law) is one possessed by a relatively large enterprise and extended over markets and commodities important enough that a large venture would be needed to invade the field. It is in such instances that substitute commodities are likely to be controlled by the monopolist rather than by others, that invaders of the monopolized area would have to ship from considerable distances or from outside the country, that concerns in other industries may hestitate to challenge the monopoly for fear of retaliation, and that entry into the monopolized business by newcomers is difficult because of the size of the venture, the complications of the technology, and the handicaps inherent in inexperience and lack of suitable business connections. Though there are exceptions, the big company rather than the little is likely to convert a large percentage of production into effective monopoly power.

There is no need to repeat here the arguments from both theory and experience which support the view that concerns posssing monopoly power use it characteristically against the public interest. This kind of bigness is rarely serviceable to the public, and in the few cases where we regard it as inevitable we surround it with public utility controls to prevent abuse.

But monopoly is relatively uncommon as a nation-wide phenomenon in important industries. The environment is unsuited to it because of our anti-trust laws, the dynamic fluidity of our economy and our technology, and the rapid growth in the size of our markets. It exists here and there in localized markets and in specialized small industries, usually with degrees of power that are sharply limited in the ways that have already been discussed.

Oligopoly Power

A much more common condition is oligopoly—that is, dominance of a market or industry by a few concerns rather than one. Information about the prevalence of oligopolies is voluminous but faulty. Most of it consists of statistics showing, for a given date, the proportion of the total shipments of a product or the total shipments by an industry which originated in the largest four or the largest eight business enterprises engaged in that line of production.

For the year 1937, the Temporary National Economic Committee reported the degree of concentration prevailing for 1,807 products which accounted for more than half of the total value of manufacturing production for that year.[1] For more than half of these products, with two-thirds of the total value of all of them, four concerns or fewer produced 70 percent or more of the total national output.

For the year 1947 the Secretary of Commerce reported to Congress[2] the percentage of the total shipments of each census industry which originated in the four largest concerns primarily engaged in that industry. In 46 industries, which accounted for 7.66 percent of the total value of manufacturing shipments, the four largest companies supplied more than 75 percent of the total. In an additional 104 industries, which provided an additional 14.2 percent of the total value, the percentage shipped by the four largest companies fell between 50 and 75 percent. Thus four companies or fewer furnished half or more of the ship-

---

[1] Temporary National Economic Committee Monograph No. 27, *The Structure of Industry,* (Washington, D.C., Government Printing Office, 1941) p. 275.

[2] Letter from Charles Sawyer, Secretary of Commerce to Emanuel Celler, Chairman, Subcommittee on Study of Monopoly, House Judiciary Committee, December 1, 1949. The data are reproduced in Federal Trade Commission, *Report on Changes in Concentration in Manufacturing, 1935 to 1947 and 1950,* (Washington, D. C., Government Printing Office, 1954) Appendix D.

ments in 150 industries representing 21.86 percent of the total value of shipments.[1]

The following were among the industries showing high percentages of concentration:

Industry	Percentage of total shipments made by largest 4 companies
Primary aluminum	100 (3 companies)
Aluminum rolling and drawing	94.2
Electric lamps	91.8
Cigarettes	90.6
Flat glass	88.1
Gypsum products	84.6
Matches	82.7
Cork products	80.7
Rubber footwear	80.7
Salt	80.5
Hard-surfaced floor coverings	80.3
Typewriters	79.4
Soap and glycerin	79.0
Synthetic fibers	78.4
Tin cans and other tinware	77.8
Corn products	77.2
Sewing machines	77.1
Tires and inner tubes	76.6

---

[1] These percentages are based on totals that do not include twelve industries in which there were insuperable statistical difficulties in basing estimates upon value of shipments. For these industries, estimates were computed in terms of value added by manufacture. Of the total value added by these twelve industries, two percent fell in three small industries in which the largest four concerns supplied more than 75 percent of the total, and 46 percent fell in three more industries in which the largest four supplied more than 50 percent of the total.

Although figures like these are the best we have, they are not wholly satisfactory. The census definition of an industry often departs widely from the kind of industry that has meaning in the market place. In some cases, the industry that is statistically recorded in the census is too broad to fit the facts of competition. In many instances, though figures are available for the nation as a whole, the census does not disclose production by regions; and even where regional figures are available, there is typically very little information about the amount of cross-shipment between regions. Therefore we are usually forced to measure concentration for the whole country, although the competitive market in some industries is regional or even local. In such cases the national total may show a degree of concentration lower than actually prevails in important regions or localities. Again, the census definition of an industry may cover products that do not actually compete with one another. The motor vehicle industry, as defined by the census, includes not only the manufacturers of automobiles but also the makers of various kinds of replacement parts. The actual concentration of automobile production in 1947 was very high; most of the new cars were produced by three companies. But after the total size of the industry had been increased in the census figures by adding the value of the automotive equipment produced by many other concerns, the census reports indicated that the largest four companies controlled only 55.7 percent of the industry. No information is available to show in how many cases concentration of control in a significant market is underestimated because of such an over-broad definition of the industry.

In other cases the industry as defined by the census is too narrow to reflect the competitive facts. In the cane-sugar refining industry, for example, the largest four companies produced 69.9 percent of the total output in 1947. In the beet sugar industry, the corresponding percentage was 68.4 percent, and in corn products refining it was 77.2 percent. Thus each of these three industries appears to have a high degree of concentration. For most uses, however, cane and beet sugar are indistinguishable, and for many uses the glucose which is one of the main products of the corn products refining industry is a satisfactory substitute for sugar. It is probable, therefore, that the four leading producers of cane sugar encounter competition not only from the smaller cane sugar refineries but also from concerns, both large and small, in the other two industries. Thus it is probable that the figures on concentration of sugar production are grossly overstated. There is a similar overstatement of concentration whenever an industry's products compete with close substitutes produced by different companies in other industries.

To determine the extent of such overstatements is not easy. Since most substitutes are not as interchangeable as cane and beet sugar, difficult problems of judgment arise in deciding how far the competition of substitutes should be allowed to modify concentration ratios. Moreover, a substitute affords additional competition only when the principal producers of it are different companies from those already covered by the concentration ratio. In considering any single instance of concentration, one can ascertain the names of the leading producers of the relevant substitutes; but such specific inquiry is not feasible in developing a picture of concentration throughout the manufacturing economy. Since the census figures do not disclose the names of the leading companies, we cannot tell how widely the competition of substitutes is indicative of more competition. 1088842

But even if the names of the big companies were available, interpretation of the figures as to concentration would still be hard. In many cases companies that are nominally independent are bound together by interlocking stock ownership, by patent licenses, by agency contracts, or by other kinds of arrangements that prevent them from competing with each other. Magnesium and aluminum, for example, are substitutes in many uses. Therefore it would appear logical for the availability of magnesium to diminish the importance of the concentrated control of aluminum. But before the second world war the sole producer of magnesium had agreed with the principal aluminum producer to limit the quantity of magnesium to be produced and to set a price for magnesium which was high enough to offset much of its advantage over aluminum. While this arrangement existed, no significant competition between the two metals was possible.[1]

Thus figures on industrial concentration are not very reliable. The concentration that significantly affects competition is probably higher in many cases and probably lower in many cases than the published figures indicate. Nevertheless, we may safely infer that there are many important instances in which a few large companies control most of the output in a competitive field.

Like monopoly, oligopoly may appear in large markets or small ones, but is significant primarily where the markets and the oligopolists are large. But apart from these matters of scale, oligopoly is a complex phenomenon, with important variations in significance.

There are many patterns of oligopoly. The "few" enterprises among which most of the sales in the market are divided may be only two, as in the tin can industry, or as many as twenty-two, as in the petroleum industry, or any number in between. Within the oligopolistic group, one enterprise may be substantially larger than the rest, two or more enterprises may be of approximately

---

[1]*U.S. v. Aluminum Company of America, et al.; U.S. v. American Magnesium Corporation, et al.; U.S. v. Dow Chemical Company, et al.* Indictments in all three cases were returned on January 30, 1941, and the principal defendants pleaded nolo contendere and were fined in all three cases on April 15, 1942. See also a companion civil case, *U.S. v. Aluminum Company of America,* complaint April 15, 1942, consent decree the same day.

equal size, two groups of enterprises may differ in size, or there may be a stair-step sequence from largest to smallest. There may or may not be in the industry a considerable number of companies too small to be regarded as part of the oligopoly. The members of the oligopoly group may be closely associated in various ways, for example by exchange of technology, or each member may keep its own secrets and pursue its own advantage separately. The oligopolistic companies may be similar or markedly different in their degrees of vertical integration and in the extent to which their vertically integrated operations must be supplemented by purchase or sale in the open market. They may also be similar or different in their business strategies—the relative emphasis they place upon research, exploitation of patents, sales effort, relations with distributors, cost reduction, liquidity, and other aspects of business management. Finally, there may be many different patterns as to the diversity of each concern's operations outside the oligopolistic industry, the importance each concern attaches to the industry as compared with its other activities, the frequency with which each concern finds itself in contact with the others in the various industries in which it operates, and the relative size attained by each concern in the aggregate of its operations.

The effect of oligopoly upon competition is not uniform, partly because of such variations in pattern. In some instances, though apparently not many, the competition within an oligopoly appears to resemble in kind and intensity that which economists attribute to an industry composed of small producers. More common appears to be a limited competition, centered upon product development and sales effort but avoiding direct rivalry as to price. In cases in which the same concerns are prominent together in a considerable number of industries, each may consider that the possible gains from successful competition in any one industry are small in comparison with the risks that conflict in one industry will spread to others; and therefore each may avoid the temptation to compete where competition looks profitable, and thus avoid the incommensurate dangers of general combat. In some instances the desire to live and let live develops into tacit, if not explicit, agreement.

Confronted with these different types of oligopoly behavior, one cannot make a single sweeping judgment as to the significance of oligopolies. There is no reason to condemn oligopolies that are fully competitive. Concerted action by the oligopolists to eliminate competition can be regarded as nonfunctional and objectionable, whether the unison of the big companies has been achieved by formal agreement or merely by separate decisions not to compete. When the competition of the oligopolists has become limited and has been diverted from price competition to other forms of competition, the significance of the change is hotly disputed. Since this aspect of oligopoly must be discussed in considering the case that is made for big business, further consideration of it will be deferred to the next chapter.

Power Derived from Sheer Size

Whereas both monopoly and oligopoly power are derived from a large percentage of the market, a third type of business power rests, not upon a percentage of a market total, but upon the sheer size of the business enterprise. Power derived from bigness rather than percentage has had little place in economic theory, but it is familiar to most of us, nevertheless. We refer to price leadership, and in doing so we usually expect that a large company will be the leader. We refer to the price policies of a big company; and in doing so we imply that the company enjoys an unusually wide range of discretion. We refer to an "independent" business, by which we usually mean a small enterprise whose independence is doubtful. In many industries we take it for granted that certain large companies will devise standard contract forms which other companies will accept or that certain large companies will expect and get preferential treatment. Such concepts and expectations exist about industries that are not thought of as monopolistic or signficantly oligopolistic.

Discussion of the power of big companies has been confused by the fact that there is no general agreement as to the degree of bigness that is significant. When the term big business is used, it sometimes means companies employing more than 10,000 people and sometimes companies employing more than 500 people. Sometimes it means companies with more than a billion dollars in assets, sometimes companies with more than one hundred million, and sometimes companies with more than five million. Sometimes it means the largest hundred companies; sometimes the largest two hundred; sometimes the largest five hundred; and sometimes the largest thousand. Sometimes the concept of bigness is applied industry by industry, so that a company engaged in a small industry may be described as big, regardless of its total size, if in that industry it is decidedly larger than its competitors. Sometimes the concept is applied to the whole economy or to a broad segment thereof, so that a concern is described as big only if it carries on a substantial part of all industrial activity.

What is true of billion dollar companies is not necessarily true of five million dollar ones, and leadership of the whole economy may involve a different kind of power from that displayed by the leading firm in a small industry. Thus these ambiguities in the concept of big business have fostered confusion about the relation between bigness and power.

The bigness that is relevant to other types of power than monopoly or oligopoly is best measured by a comparison of the total size of different business enterprises in all their activities. By this measure, companies are relatively big if they have more of the assets, sales, or employment of the economy than other companies. Since various degrees of power may attach to different degrees of bigness, a definition of big companies as those included in a stated number of the largest or those having more than a stated amount of assets, sales, or employment is an arbitrary simplification.

The policy of competition applies primarily to the fields of manufacture and distribution. It is, therefore, to these fields that measures of bigness are particularly appropriate. In manufacturing 40.5 percent of the value of all output in 1950 was produced by the 200 largest companies; 33.3 percent by the 100 largest; 26.6 percent by the 50 largest; and 11.4 percent by the 5 largest.[1] There were few large concerns. In 1952 there were about 3,200 manufacturing companies with assets of $5,000,000 or over. Of these, about 1,700 had assets of $10,000,000 or over; 389, assets of $50,000,000 or over; 219, assets of $100,000,000 or over; 94, assets of a quarter of a billion or over; 36, assets of half a billion or over; and 18, assets above a billion dollars.[2]

---

[1] Federal Trade Commission, *Report on Changes in Concentration in Manufacturing, 1935 to 1947 and 1950, op. cit.,* p. 17. *Fortune* magazine has estimated (issue of July, 1955. p. 96) that in 1954 the largest 500 manufacturing and mining companies in the United States had 56 percent of the assets of all American industrial companies, half of the industrial output, 44 percent of the industrial work force, and two-thirds of the net earnings of all industrial firms. As used in this estimate, the term industrial excludes utility, transportation, finance, construction, trade, and service companies. The 500 companies covered do not include concerns, such as Ford and Lever Brothers, which do not publish sales figures.

[2] Information for companies with assets in excess of $50,000,000 was supplied by the Federal Trade Commission on the basis of the number of companies of the various size groups covered by the Quarterly Financial Reports issued by the Commission jointly with the Securities and Exchange Commission. For 1951, the Internal Revenue Service reported 373 corporations with assets in excess of $50,000,000, of which 199 had assets in excess of $100,000,000. For the five million and ten million dollar categories, the estimates are based upon the Bureau of Internal Revenue's

The power that is derived from bigness probably attaches primarily to these companies. Some portions of that power relate directly to the sheer bigness of the largest companies, their importance in the economy as a whole, and the frequency with which they encounter each other. Thus a billion dollar company may be powerful because its assets are worth a billion dollars. Other aspects of power relate primarily to the relative size of big and little companies. These are best measured, not by the bigness of the big, but by the difference between the big and the little. Thus a fifty million dollar company may be powerful because its suppliers are only one-fiftieth as large. Still other aspects of power relate to the attainment of a size large enough to undertake expensive projects, and show themselves chiefly as a handicap suffered by concerns that are below some relevant level of size. Thus any enterprise big enough to have a cost accounting system may have an advantage over an enterprise too small to do so.

Pre-war Japan provides a good example of the power that accrues to large enterprises when a few of them have acquired important positions in every part of the economy.[1] A small number of corporate combines, collectively known as the Zaibatsu, or money clique, dominated the Japanese economy. There were few examples of monopoly, for in most important industries most of the Zaibatsu combines were in decorous competition with one

Statistics of Income, 1951, Part 2, in which the numbers are slightly larger than in the Commission's corresponding figures for 1952. Discrepancies between the two sets of figures are partly due to different methods of classifying corporations and consolidating reports and partly to the fact that, in the Quarterly Financial Reports, corporations which had attained assets of more than $5,000,000 since 1949 were covered only on a sampling basis.

[1] *Report of the Mission on Japanese Combines, Part I.* (Washington, D. C., U. S. Department of State, 1946).

another. But whatever industry one examined was organized as an oligopoly drawn from the same few concerns. Collectively these combines controlled Japanese credit, the opportunity to go into business, and the rate and character of industrial expansion. Except on the rare occasions when they clashed with the military authorities, they also dominated the economic aspects of Japanese politics. They determined the content of Japanese laws relating to business organization and trade. The two largest took turns in selecting the Minister of Finance, and others had similar perquisites elsewhere in the government. A particular combine drew its young executives from a particular university; and a young man once employed by one Zaibatsu company was committed to that company for life, since no other combine would thereafter offer him employment. Although this was not monopoly power as we understand monopoly, it was certainly not open opportunity and competitive private enterprise.

The Zaibatsu illustrate the extreme possibilities of power derived from bigness, just as one company's production of the entire output of an important industry, where there are no substitutes and no opportunities for others to enter, illustrates the extreme possibility of monopoly power. The United States has neither type of extreme case. But just as we have oligopolies and partial monopolies, so we have lesser degrees of power based upon bigness.[1]

Some degrees and kinds of bigness are functionally useful, but these will be discussed in the next chapter as a part of the case for big business. Here it is appropriate to consider aspects of the power of large enterprises which do not improve the function-

---

[1]The power derived from bigness is more fully discussed in an article by Corwin D. Edwards entitled "The Conglomerate Enterprise," which appears in the National Bureau of Economic Research's volume, *Business Concentration and Price Policy,* (Princeton, N. J., Princeton University Press, 1955).

ing of the economic system. In some instances their effect is merely to transfer risks and costs. In other instances they actually retard or limit the performance of the economy.

Big companies enjoy substantial buying advantages over small companies. A big customer may buy so much of the total output of its supplier that the supplier cannot afford to lose the sale and therefore treats the big buyer with special consideration. When still larger, the big company buys certain components of its products in quantities as great as the total output of an efficient establishment producing those components. As the size of the buyer increases, more of the components come to be bought in such quantities. For each component, when the necessary quantity is reached, vertical integration becomes possible. But the large company does not need to produce its own raw materials in order to get advantage from being big enough to do so. By threatening to supply itself, it may induce its suppliers to give it special discounts and perhaps may buy more cheaply than it could make. If its consumption of materials is large enough, it may produce a minor part of what it uses and may thus intensify the threat of self-sufficiency and at the same time obtain information about costs with which it can bargain for price reductions more effectively. Though the law against price discrimination forbids certain types of favoritism, it does not eliminate all such buying advantages. It is sometimes violated, and it is often evaded. A large buyer may take the entire output of a particular seller, so that the low buying price is not a discriminatory one; or it may buy a component of a different grade and quality from that sold to others, so that the law does not apply; or it may merely obtain preferential treatment, so that it has less trouble than its competitors as to credit terms, variation in quality, delayed deliveries, adequate supplies in time of shortage, allowances for defective merchandise, and similar matters.

The large company may choose to integrate vertically. In doing so, it may, of course find ways of increasing the efficiency of the production process or of eliminating overcapitalization, unnecessary sales expenses, or other excessive financial burdens. But apart from such economically beneficial results, it may use partial integration to shift costs from itself to others. If it uses more of a raw material than it produces, it may keep its own output of the material steady, although demand for the finished product fluctuates, by adjusting its open market purchases. Such a policy shifts the risks of instability to the nonintegrated supplier. Similarly, if the vertically integrated company produces more of a raw material than it consumes, it can derive advantages from its position as supplier to its own competitiors. It may give preference to its own fabricating plants when materials are scarce. Moreover, if the partially integrated concern is big enough to influence prices at the various vertical levels, it may squeeze its fabricating competitors by raising the price of the raw materials relative to that of the fabricated commodity or squeeze the nonintegrated producer of raw material by lowering the price of the raw material and thus increasing the fabricator's share of the sales dollar.

The large company may diversify its operations, thereby minimizing the impact of any single market or product upon its profits. Though the company's stability is thereby enhanced, its responsiveness to market forces may be reduced. Because the large diversified companies are likely to have many points of contact in different markets, there is an incentive for each of them to avoid widespread conflict by maintaining the status quo in any particular market, in disregard of special opportunities and pressures there. Moreover, the management of a large diversified company is not likely to be acutely aware of the circumstances that prevail in each market where the company operates. Regard for the status quo and ignorance of particular markets both tend to diminish the company's responsiveness to changes of costs and of demand.

44

More important for our present purpose, diversification may give the large company decisive power over smaller and more specialized enterprises. If the diversified company cuts prices severely in any one area, it can destroy a local enterprise without substantially reducing its own profits. This is the procedure by which some monopolies consolidated their power. Similarly, if the large diversified company cuts prices severely upon any one commodity, it can destroy specialized producers in that line while it offsets its losses by profits in other lines. Consequently, the large diversified enterprise holds the smaller specialized enterprise at its mercy.[1]

---

[1] T. K. Quinn, former vice-president of General Electric Company, has illustrated this possibility as follows (in *I Quit Monster Business,* a pamphlet privately published in 1948, p. 4): "I have before me the annual report for 1947 of the General Motors Corporation . . . For want of unrevealed departmental figures, I shall estimate the electric home appliance business of the company at $100,000,000, which is a maximum figure. Its profit on that business, if up to its average, would be $10,000,000. By itself this $10,000,000 is a very large amount, but in relation to the total net income of $375,517,000.00 it is less than 3 percent. In all probability the net profits on the corporation's Frigidaire and other home appliance business was less than 2 percent of the total profits. The whole electrical appliance industry, which is generally thought of as being big and important, is much smaller than the automobile business. The bosses of the company could decide tomorrow that they would like to double or treble their appliance business and therefore reduce appliance prices by approximately 10 percent or enough to entirely wipe out the profit on that part of the total business. This action might be applauded nationally as a stroke of industrial statesmanship and it would cost no more than 3 percent of the company's total profit. By thus doing business on home appliances at cost, without profit, or if necessary going below cost, the company could within a matter of months wipe out those thousands of manufacturing, distributing and retailing competitors who have no other departments to absorb losses. The cost of this elimination of competitors would hardly be noticeable in the overall figures of the corporation. General Motors would,

A company possessing such power does not need to use it, or even contemplate using it, in order to bring the possibility vividly to the minds of those against whom it may be used. Consequently, an attitude of one-way respect may develop between large companies and small ones. Except where there is risk that complaint might lead to intervention by the government through anti-trust investigation or Congressional hearing, a large company need not carefully consider whether its commercial and financial decisions will be liked by its smaller competitors. Small companies often find it necessary to give anxious thought to the opinions which their business policies may arouse in their larger competitors. It is not wise to provoke a big company sufficiently to run the risk of discipline or destruction.[1]

---

of course, deny any intention of crushing competition but this does not in the least change the fact that the corporation is in a position to do so and at almost negligible proportionate cost."

[1] A striking public expression of such an attitude may be found in the hearings of the Temporary National Economic Committee, in testimony by the President of Riverside Metal Co. in May, 1939:

"Mr. Cox: And your company follows the prices which are announced by American Brass?

Mr. Randall: That is correct.

Mr. Cox: So when they reduce the price you have to reduce the price?

Mr. Randall: Well, we don't have to, but we do.

Mr. Cox: And When they raise the price you raise the price?

Mr. Randall: That is correct . . .

Mr. Arnold: You exercise no individual judgment as to the price you charged for your product, then, in a situation?

Mr. Randall: Well, I think that is about what it amounts to; yes, sir . . . Of course, as Mr. Cox first stated, the industry is one of price leadership, and a small company like ours, making less than $1\frac{1}{2}$ percent of the total, we have to follow . . .

Mr. Arnold: When you say you have to follow, you don't mean anybody told you you had to follow?

Mr. Randall: No, sir; I don't mean that at all.

46

The large manufacturer may exercise a considerable degree of control over the distribution of its products. In the background lies the possibility that manufacturers' outlets may take over the wholesaling and retailing functions or that exclusive distributorships may be granted to more docile distributors. In the light of such possibilities, the policies of distributors may be prescribed by the large manufacturer. A stated minimum of promotional service may be required; payment for a part of the manufacturer's advertising may be exacted; minimum quotas of sales may be

---

Mr. Arnold: But you have a feeling that something might happen if you didn't?

Mr. Randall: I don't know what would happen.

Mr. Cox: You don't want to find out, do you?

The Chairman: Well, as a matter of fact, Mr. Randall, if the American Brass Co. raised the price, would the Brass Co. consult you about raising it?

Mr. Randall: No sir; not at all.

The Chairman: You would, however, follow them without exercising any independent judgment as to whether or not it was desirable?

Mr. Randall: That is correct.

Mr. Cox: We have here a memorandum which the Department took from Mr. Gahagan's file, dated August 30, 1937, and entitled 'Memorandum of Conversation with Mr. Randall of Riverside Metal Co.' . . . . in the first paragraph this statement occurs:

"He"—referring, I assume, to you—"stated that he felt the attitude of the American Brass Co. was uncalled for, and that they should reduce the price of beryllium copper alloys, but that he did not dare take such a step himself, as American Brass were too strong and could make it uncomfortable for him in other directions."

Do you remember making that statement to Mr. Gahagan?

Mr. Randall: No; I do not. I'm sorry, I do not.

Mr. Arnold. You might have made it, might you not?

Mr. Randall: It is quite possible, I don't recall."

See *Investigation of the Concentration of Economic Power, hearings before the Temporary National Economic Committee,* (Washington, D.C., Government Printing Office, 1939) Part 5, pp. 2086-2090.

set; resale prices may be fixed; the handling of competing products may be severely limited or entirely forbidden; the handling of the manufacturer's full line may be required; and the nominally independent distributor may be required to operate in a building with a given size and layout, and to decorate it in a given way. In extreme instances distributors have been expected to accept shipments that were not ordered, and to distribute publications expressing the manufacturer's political and social views. As in the case of price discrimination, the anti-trust laws have specifically forbidden some forms of control, particularly tying contracts and certain exclusive dealing arrangements, but have not destroyed the large concern's pervasive authority.

Through its control over distribution, the large concern may transfer to the distributor or the buyer a considerable number of miscellaneous risks and costs which might logically fall upon either party to a transaction. Big companies often devise standard contract forms which place upon others whatever losses and costs arise from delayed shipment, damage in transit, change in freight rates, and similar matters; and smaller concerns which buy from the large ones habitually accept the conditions of such standard forms without change.

The large company derives advantage from its sheer financial strength. There appear to be cases in which particular large companies have been given preferential access to the funds of certain large banks. But apart from such favored positions, the scale upon which a large company spends and invests money may be a source of advantage. When a big company bids against smaller ones for inventions, administrators, or productive facilities, it can outspend its rivals. This type of advantage is especially important to the large company in assuring itself supplies and facilities that will be needed in the future. U. S. Steel Corp., for example, acquired the most important iron ore deposits of the Mesabi Range at an early date, and to this day has larger reserves of high grade accessible ore there than the other steel companies. If Mesabi ore were the only ore available, U. S. Steel probably would have a monopoly of high grade ore in a few more years. Now that ore is becoming scarce, U. S. Steel Corp., and Bethlehem Steel Corp., have found it possible to spend large sums in finding and developing other ore deposits in South America. The smaller steel companies are not big enough to do the same thing individually, and the ones that are developing new ore supplies in Canada have found it necessary to pool their resources for the venture. Of course it was important to the public that somebody do this expensive exploration and development, and whoever did it would have had to be big enough for the task. But because of the differences in size, the new facilities found are not equally open to all, as they presumably would have been if the exploratory ventures had been undertaken primarily by ore merchants or by all steel companies cooperatively. Instead the future ore supply of the large companies is reasonably well assured and that of some of the smaller companies is precarious.[1]

Large companies have special political advantage, obtained primarily by spending money. Initially the large company is under suspicion in politics because it is big. However, through campaign contributions it may be able to offset this disadvantage. Its most significant source of political power, however, is its maintenance of a staff at the seat of government. It finds out what issues important to it are developing in government offices,

---

[1] See Federal Trade Commission, *Report to the Anti-trust Subcommittee of the Judiciary Committee of the House of Representatives on the Control of Iron Ore.* (Washington D. C., Government Printing Office, 1952.) One important ore merchant, M. A. Hanna Company, has a 27 percent interest in the Canadian venture. Its affiliate, National Steel Corp., (of which Hanna owns 27.18 percent of the stock) has a 20 percent interest. The remaining 53 percent is shared among four steel companies. Republic (25%), Armco (10%), Youngstown (10%), and Wheeling (8%).

who will decide them, and when he probably will act. It assembles facts and argument relevant to the issues, prepares them carefully, and presents them to the proper person, neither too early to be remembered nor to late to be considered. Such activities by large concerns have become so general that a small business has been facetiously defined as one too small to have a full-time Washington representative. Though some small concerns carry on similar programs through trade associations, the interests of small enterprises suffer frequently because argument on their behalf has not been made or has been presented at the wrong place or time or has been badly prepared. As the decisions of government have come to deal more intimately with matters that directly affect business success, the political advantage of the large company has become more important.[1]

Large companies also tend to have special advantages in litigation. They can disregard the costs of preparing and contesting lawsuits, and thus can fully exploit their legal rights. When dealing with smaller companies they can stretch their legal rights by bargaining based upon their greater willingness to litigate. They can harass inconvenient small rivals by multiple lawsuits. They can use contracts to convert a temporary legal advantage into an enduring status.

The patent policies of certain large companies illustrate these possibilities. A patent is a 17-year grant of exclusive rights to an invention, which may be employed either to prevent others from using the invention or to license use by others under restrictions

---

[1] Various government agencies to protect small business have been established from time to time by the Federal Government in an effort to reduce advantages enjoyed by the larger companies. They have had to do with specific programs, not with the broad range of business interests in government activity. Even in their specifically assigned fields, they appear to have had substantial effect only where they were supported by statutory discrimination in favor of small business.

and subject to royalties imposed by the owner of the patent. Anyone who uses the invention without the owner's permission may be sued for infringement and required to pay damages; but in such a suit the defendant may challenge the validity of the patent. Courts often find that patents were improperly issued, thus opening the alleged invention to use by everyone.

A large business enterprise may own hundreds or even thousands of patents, for it not only obtains patents upon the results of research by its employees but also buys patents from inventors who find the large patent-owner the best or even the only market for their inventions. With many patents and willingness to litigate, it enjoys power substantially greater than the power of an individual patent owner. It has little to fear from expiration of its patents, since new ones are constantly being acquired. It has little risk that its patents will be invalidated in the courts. Other large companies will seldom attack the weak patents lest there be retaliation. Licensees can be required to acknowledge the validity of all the patents, weak as well as strong. Small companies cannot readily carry the burden of lawsuits covering many assorted charges of infringement even if they believe that they can eventually win all the suits. Moreover, patent litigation exposes a small defendant to two risks, first, that during the pendency of a suit for heavy damages, the contingent liability created by the suit will injure the small concern's credit; and second, that customers will be lost because of the possibility that they might be sued for contributory infringement.[1]

---

[1] To assist in, or bring about, the infringement of a valid patent is to incur liability for damages. Purchase of goods that infringe the patent has been held to fall within this rule. If a patent owner begins suits based on such purchases, buyers are unlikely to continue buying at the risk of lawsuits, even if they are confident they could win. To hold its trade, the concern charged with infringement probably must guarantee its customers against damage claims and the costs of suit. But the contingent liability created by such guarantees can be enormous.

The impact of the big company's patent control is broader than could be exercised with a single patent. Wherever technological alternatives are known or can be devised, the bit of technology monopolized under a single patent need not convey monopoly of a productive activity or of an industry. But a big company often tries to patent all the ways of producing the same effect; and if it succeeds, it acquires a monopoly of the effect as well as of the means. Patents upon the technological alternatives which it does not wish to employ may be used to block the development of these methods by other companies, and thus a market or an industry may be monopolized.

In the dealings between large and small companies, extensive patent control by the large is sometimes used to shut the small ones out of attractive lines of business, but more often to impose upon the small a close control of their marketing activities Licenses are likely to fix prices, impose production quotas, and allocate territories and types of commodities. In the dealings of one big company with another, patents perform a different function. Since each large company is likely to have technology that could be useful to the other, reflected in patents that could be used to harass the other, the patent agreement tends to take the form of a comprehensive exchange of patent rights and technical information. In such an agreement, care is usually taken to allocate products and fields, so that competition based upon the pooled technology is avoided; but within its own field the large company is likely to be left to exploit its patent position as it chooses. Thus patent licensing may be used to eliminate competition among the big, to strengthen each big company against outsiders, and to reduce small companies to enduring positions of technological and commercial subservience.

The ability of large business enterprises to work together easily and thereby strengthen one another is not limited to the exploitation of patents. It is a general advantage of the big over the small.

Through reciprocal buying two large companies may assure to each other whatever profit and enhancement of strength can be obtained by having a large concern as an assured customer. By joint ownership of productive facilities or transportation agencies, two or more big companies may avoid competition with each other and may pool their resources and their technology to make a new venture easier and to exclude others from control over it.

Big companies can also agree to set aside competition more easily than small companies. Among small concerns, such an agreement in a substantial market must include many participants and hence is hard to make, hard to conceal, and hard to enforce. Among a few large companies, agreement can be more informal and inconspicuous and is more likely to be respected. Moreover, big companies have peculiar opportunities to strengthen their position by allocation agreements which would usually be useless for small companies. The groundwork for an allocation of fields is often laid in the investment policies of large enterprises before there is formal agreement. Investments in new lines of business or in fields where competition is weak usually looks more attractive than investment which directly challenges powerful rivals. Thus big companies may tend to avoid markets and products to which other big companies are committed. But since new technologies may cross each other, such avoidance may not avert competition on industrial frontiers. If lines of growth can be channeled, by patent agreements or otherwise, aspirations to grow and desires not to compete may be reconciled. Each big company may come to have a recognized field, and may undertake not to poach in the fields of others. The effect of allocation is to eliminate competition among the large enterprises that participate and thus to leave each one free to dominate its own markets if it can control or eliminate the smaller concerns that are engaged there. With advantages over small companies derived from buying strength, vertical integration, diversification, control over distributors, financial strength, and special opportunities in litigation and politics, large enterprises often have no need to fear competition from smaller ones. Where this is true, an allocation agreement which removes competition by other large companies is sufficient to assure the power of the big concern.

Power that is not functionally necessary and power that is abused are to be found in monopoly and oligopoly (both of which, when significant, are associated with bigness) and also in bigness itself. Even if the power of monopolies and oligipolies were destroyed by action under the anti-trust laws, the sheer bigness of big companies would still give them power that is capable of abuse and is in fact abused.[1] This is the essence of the political and economic case against big business. But it is not a complete case.

The Anti-Trust Record of Large Companies

Thus far the analysis has proceeded in qualitative terms. Types of power have been described and appraised, but no effort has been made to determine whether they are common or exceptional. How often does monopoly appear? How often does oligopolistic concentration create an anti-competitive exercise of oligopoly power? How frequently do the few big companies have power that is primarily non-functional? How often do they use it abusively to collaborate among themselves and to coerce smaller companies? The strength of the case against big business depends largely upon the answers to these questions.

---

[1] In anti-trust proceedings the effects of bigness have sometimes been treated as manifestations of monopoly or of a purpose to monopolize. Thus they have been subjected to the remedies of the anti-trust laws, when otherwise there might have been no legal remedy. By this process, however, the significance of bigness has been obscured and clear thinking about public policy has been made more difficult.

Because of our anti-trust laws, the answers need not be left to mere opinion. Though some of the uses of power that have been discussed are violative of no law, those that are collusive or monopolistic in purpose or effect impair competition in ways that the laws forbid; and from time to time these have been discovered and prosecuted. The character and frequency of such cases may be regarded not only as evidence showing the prevalence of the activities directly questioned but also as a sample of conduct that may suggest the nature and frequency of the abuse of types of power derived from sheer bigness, that are not open to direct challenge in the courts.

There is a possibility, of course, that some law violations have remained undetected and that some decisions in the courts have been mistaken; but a private commentator can scarcely expect to improve upon the judicial process in ascertaining facts that are involved in controversy.

Accordingly, the decisions of the courts and of the Federal Trade Commission have been examined in an effort to ascertain how often our largest industrial companies have violated the anti-trust laws and what has been the nature of the violations.

The companies selected for study are the fifty largest industrial concerns as listed by A. D. H. Kaplan[1] for the year 1948. For each of these companies a list was developed[2] showing the cases instituted by the Department of Justice in which the company (a) was found guilty after trial (and appeal, if any) or

---

[1] In *Big Enterprise in a Competitive System, op. cit.,* p. 153.

[2] From the Department of Justice a list was obtained showing the cases in which the company had been named as a defendant. An authoritative summary (the Federal Anti-trust Laws, with Summary of Cases Instituted by the United States, Commerce Clearing House, Chicago, 1952) was examined to ascertain the disposition of each case. Where disposition as to the designated defendant could not be ascertained from the summary, specific inquiry was made at the Department of Justice.

(b) pleaded nolo contendere[1] and was fined or (c) accepted a consent degree. To this were added the cases pending against the company without final decision. Where more than one case was instituted concerning the same situation (for example a criminal proceeding and a civil suit for injunction), the related cases were grouped together and treated as a single proceeding. A second list was developed for each company showing the cases in which the Federal Trade Commission had found the company guilty of violating the Clayton Act or of monopolitic practices forbidden by the Federal Trade Commission Act[2] and in which this finding had not been set aside on appeal.[3] Pending cases of the same kind were added to this list also.

As presented in the Appendix, the tabulation of these cases provides a minimum statement of each company's violations of law.

Few cases are covered involving subsidiaries of the largest fifty companies. The fifty companies listed had a total of substantially more than 2,000 subsidiaries in 1948.[4] To search the records of

---

[1] A plea of nolo contendere, entered in a criminal proceeding, states the defendant's intention not to contest the case but to consent to the imposition of an appropriate penalty. It differs from a plea of guilty by not formally admitting the defendant's guilt.

[2] *The Clayton Act,* which forbids certain kinds of price discrimination, exclusive dealing, acquisition of corporate stock or assets, and interlocking directorates, is technically part of the anti-trust laws. *The Federal Trade Commission Act* is not. Unfair competitive practices, forbidden by the latter statute, include not only a variety of offenses characterized by misrepresentation and similar breaches of commercial ethics, but also conspiracies to fix prices, efforts to intimidate or destroy competitors, and similar anti-competitive schemes. Only the latter type of violation of the Federal Trade Commission Act was included in the list.

[3] A list of these cases was obtained from the Federal Trade Commission.

[4] Federal Trade Commission, *A List of 1,000 Large Manufacturing Companies, Their Subsidiaries and Affiliates,* (1948).

more than 1,200 Sherman Act cases and of 49 bound volumes of decisions by the Federal Trade Commission for each of these 2,000 companies would have been excessively time-consuming. Accordingly attention was centered upon cases brought against the parent companies. Where the involvement of a subsidiary was a matter of common knowledge or thrust itself upon the attention of the author, the case was included;[1] but such inclusions are few, and, except for dairy products, no systematic search for cases against subsidiaries has been made.[2]

Similarly, the cases listed probably do not include various proceedings against companies that were subsequently merged with one of the largest fifty companies. Many of the largest fifty attained a considerable part of their bigness by absorbing other concerns. Where a merger involved a slight change of corporate name, the predecessor company has been regarded as a forerunner of the merged company,[3] and its law violations have been

---

[1] For example, a Sherman Act proceeding involved both Schenley Industries, which is listed in the fifty companies, and Distillers Distributing Corporation, which is a subsidiary of a company listed, Distillers Corp.—Seagrams Ltd. Both defendants are mentioned in the tabulation of cases.

[2] Since urban milksheds are relatively isolated from each other and anti-trust proceedings against dairy companies usually involve regional subsidiaries rather than national parent companies, dairy products cases under the Sherman Act were examined for inclusion of subsidiaries of National Dairy Products Co., and Federal Trade Commission cases were examined for the names of ten of the most important subsidiaries of National Dairy as well as for the name of the parent company.

[3] Problems have also arisen as to continuity in the identity of corporations that were legally dissolved. Standard Oil Company of New Jersey, for example, was dissolved in 1911; and the largest fifty companies in 1948 included several companies which were created by the dissolution. Standard Oil Co (N. J.), one of these, has been arbitrarily considered to be the successor company because of its name. Substantial identity of name has been similarly treated in other such instances.

treated as those of the merged company. But no effort has been made to trace law violations by companies whose identity disappeared in a merger. For example, Schenley Industries, one of the fifty largest, acquired seventeen distilling companies between 1933 and 1950.[1] The records of these companies under the anti-trust laws have not been examined, and if there were violations by any of them, these are not here attributed to Schenley.

Even the violations of law by the parent companies probably have been understated. The tabulation omits all cases that were dismissed, regardless of the ground for dismissal. Among the charges that were brought but not proved, some were dropped by the government, not because the charge was believed to be untrue, but for procedural reasons. For example, in some instances so much time elapsed before trial that witnesses died or became otherwise unavailable and proof was no longer possible. This was true, in particular, of certain cases instituted before the Second World War in which trial was deferred at the request of the defense agencies until after the war. Several such cases were subsequently dismissed on grounds other than lack of merit.

Moreover, information from various sources indicates that some of the large companies probably participated in arrangements that were not challenged in anti-trust proceedings but were similar to other arrangements that were challenged. An official report by the Federal Trade Commission,[2] for example, declares that Anaconda Copper Mining Company and Kennecott Copper Corp., both of which are among the largest fifty companies, were active or tacit participants in efforts to cartelize international trade in copper at various times between 1919 and

---

[1] Federal Trade Commission, *Report on Changes in Concentration in Manufacturing, op. cit,* pp. 69-70.

[2] Federal Trade Commission, *Report on the Copper Industry,* (Washington, D. C., Government Printing Office, 1947), pp. 174-250.

1939. No anti-trust proceeding upon this charge was ever undertaken by the goverment.

The tabulated cases may be regarded, therefore, as a minimum statement of the extent to which the fifty largest industrial companies have violated the anti-trust laws. In examining them, however, the reader should bear in mind that the violations differed in extent and importance. The scope of each is summarized in the tabulation. Since about fifty years is covered, it is obvious that not all of the violations prevailed at the same time.

The two tables will be found in the appendix. The discussion which follows is based upon them.

From Table I it is apparent that the integrated oil companies have been deeply and continuously involved in violations of the Sherman Act. Of the ten such companies which are among the largest fifty industrial concerns, eight have been fined or enjoined for violation of the law and another is defendant in a pending case. Nine cases charging violations by one or more of these oil companies have been won by the government, and two more are pending. The cases began with the dissolution of the old Standard Oil Company of New Jersey as a monopoly in 1911. Subsequently they have included two conspiracies to fix gasoline prices on the Pacific Coast, a conspiracy to raise gasoline prices in the Mid-Continent and East Texas fields, a conspiracy to fix jobbers' margins for gasoline in ten Middle-Western states, a conspiracy to fix the bids and select the bidders for emulsified asphalt used in state projects in Georgia, a conspiracy to monopolize the business of a nationwide combine of urban bus lines, an exclusive dealing arrangement, and a world-wide conspiracy to prevent competition between the largest oil company and one of the world's largest chemical companies. One of the two pending cases alleges that there is a conspiracy to monopolize the Pacific Coast petroleum industry. The other alleges that five American companies are parties to a world-wide cartel agreement to limit and allocate the production of crude oil and to allocate markets and fix prices for petroleum products.

The record of the two largest electrical manufacturers is also impressive. General Electric Company has lost twelve Sherman Act cases, Westinghouse five. The cases began in 1911 with a conviction of General Electric for eliminating competition in the sale of electric lamps. Three subsequent cases involving General Electric were concerned with conspiracies to monopolize the incandescent lamp industry and the fluorescent lamp industry and with payment to two Dutch companies not to compete in the United States in selling glass light bulbs. Westinghouse participated in the first two of these conspiracies. In other cases involving one or both companies the offenses were conspiracy to monopolize radio communication, conspiracy to divide the world market for all types of electrical equipment (other than lamps and radios), two more conspiracies with foreign producers to allocate business in international markets, a conspiracy to monopolize the production and sale of tungsten carbide, and four conspiracies to fix the prices of drop-out fuse cutouts, high tension cable, street lighting equipment, and electric equipment sold to West Coast public utility companies.

The record of the largest chemical company, duPont, is of a similar kind. The company began in dissolution of the old duPont powder company as a monopoly in 1913. Since that time, the successor company has lost cases involving nine violations of the Sherman Act, and it is now a defendant in two more pending cases. The adjudicated cases included conspiracy to monopolize the foreign trade of the United States in fertilizer nitrogen, conspiracy to fix the prices and limit the sales of dyestuffs, conspiracy to fix the prices of commercial explosives, conspiracies to fix the prices of sulfuric acid, chromic acid, and formic acid, conspiracy to control sales of muriatic acid, conspiracy to create a world-wide cartel controlling titanium compounds, and a world-wide conspiracy with the largest British chemical company to allocate markets for substantially all commodities produced by both companies. In the two pending cases, one charging monopolization of cellophane and the other restraint of trade by control of General Motors Company, the lower courts found in favor of duPont and the Government has appealed the decisions.

General Motors has a record of six violations, and is defendant in one pending case. The decided cases dealt with coercion of dealers to finance cars through the finance subsidiary of General Motors; conspiracies to fix the prices of ball bearings, clutch facings, friction materials, and brake linings; and participation in a conspiracy, already mentioned, to monopolize the business of certain urban bus lines. The pending case is the one concerning relations with duPont, already mentioned in connection with that company.

Through important subsidiaries, National Dairy Products has also been involved in repeated violations. Four of its milk-selling subsidiaries were fined between 1943 and 1955 for taking part in conspiracies to fix prices in Greater New York City and in the marketing areas of Louisville, Kentucky, and Cincinnati and Toledo, Ohio. Its subsidiary, Kraft, was fined three times in 1944 for taking part in conspiracies to fix the buying prices of various kinds of cheese in Wisconsin and Northern and Western New York.

For the other companies among the first fifty, the record is one of less frequent involvement. It includes, nevertheless, a considerable number of important cases. The three tire companies listed among the fifty largest were fined in 1948 for conspiracy to fix prices and allocate sales upon tires. One of them consented in 1943 to entry of a decree enjoining participation in a world-wide cartel to control latex. One or more of them were involved in four other conspiracies. The two large meat packers accepted a drastic consent decree in 1920 in a case involving conspiracy to supress competition in the purchase of livestock and the sale of dressed meats. One of them was subsequently fined twice for taking part in conspiracies to eliminate competition in the sale of mixed fertilizer. The three big tobacco companies were born in the dissolution of American Tobacco Company as a monopoly in 1911, and in 1946 were found guilty of a conspiracy to monopolize leaf tobacco buying and cigarette manufacture. The largest farm machinery manufacturer was convicted of monopolization and partially dissolved in 1918. The largest aluminum manufacturer was convicted of monopolizing virgin aluminum and subjected to a decree in 1950. The largest camera manufacturer was convicted of monopolizing photographic supplies in 1921, accepted a consent decree in 1948 in a case charging conspiracy to monpolize color-cinematography, and accepted another such decree in 1954 designed to terminate a monopoly of the development of color film. The largest paper manufacturer was enjoined in 1917 in a conspiracy to raise newsprint prices; the largest nickel company in 1948 in a conspiracy to monopolize nickel and nickel products. The third largest chemical company was involved in 1941 and 1946 in conspiracies to monopolize trade in fertilizer nitrogen and to fix prices for dyestuffs. The second and third largest automobile makers consented to decrees in 1938 designed to terminate coercion of their dealers to use their installment financing subsidiaries. Two of the large steel companies were fined and enjoined in the 1940's for participating in a conspiracy to fix the prices of stainless steel, and one of them had participated earlier in a less important price fixing conspiracy. The largest soap manufacturer was fined in 1942 for conspiring to fix soap prices, and is a defendant in a pending price fixing case that covers both soap and synthetic detergents. The largest food chain was involved in 1941 in four cases of price fixing under color of state law, was fined in 1944 for conspiracy to fix the buying prices for certain types of cheese in Western New

York, and subsequently was convicted and consented to a decree in cases charging monopolistic abuse of its mass buying and selling power. The two largest mail-order houses were involved in a recent conspiracy to prevent the rebuilding of used batteries.[1] Significant cases are pending against the largest manufacturer of telephone equipment, the largest importer of bananas, the second largest chemical company, and the two largest distillers.

In all, thirty-five of the fifty largest industrial companies have lost one or more cases, directly or through important subsidiaries, in proceedings instituted by the Department of Justice. Six others are defendants in pending cases, and nine have not been involved in any such case.[2]

Of the forty-one companies that have been defendants, twenty-four have been involved in more than one case. To nearly half of the fifty largest industrial companies, violation of the Sherman Act is more than an isolated episode. To a few it appears to be an enduring aspect of operations. If companion cases involving the same facts are treated as a single case, the Department of Justice has won a total of seventy-six cases against the defendant companies,[3] and is now prosecuting ten more.

---

[1] One of them was also a defendant in two cases based upon violation of Section 8 of the *Clayton Act* through having as directors two men who were also directors of a competitor. This case has not been included in the table, since the offense charged is unlike those in most cases instituted by the Department of Justice.

[2] Those that have not been involved are five steel companies, U. S. Steel Corp., Republic Steel Corp., Jones & Laughlin Steel Corp., National Steel Corp., and Youngstown Sheet & Tube Co.; a petroleum company, Atlantic Refining Co.; two copper companies, Anaconda Copper Mining Co., and Kennecott Copper Corp.; and one variety chain, F. W. Woolworth Co.

[3] In three instances in which companion cases were begun, the criminal case has been decided against the defendants, but the civil case is still pending. These have been counted as completed cases, since the defendants have already lost the case and the remaining controversy presumably concerns the exact terms of the injunction.

A similar picture emerges from Table II, which presents anti-monopoly proceedings by the Federal Trade Commission, that is, violations of the Clayton Act and those violations of the Federal Trade Commission Act which consisted in monopolistic practices or conspiracies to set aside competition. The violations covered are only those by parent companies, those by ten subsidiaries of National Dairy Products which were specifically checked, and those by subsidiaries of other companies which happened to come to the author's attention.

The Commission has authority to undertake preventive as well as remedial action, and some of its proceedings raise border-line issues that create controversy. Nevertheless, much of its activity has to do with violations of law as central to the competitive policy as those forbidden by the Sherman Act.

Forty-one cases are included in Table II. Of these, twenty-eight have to do with conditions similar to those that appear in Sherman Act cases; twenty-one involve conspiracy, three resale price maintenance, and four some kind of monopolistic exercise of power. In the remaining thirteen cases, the Commission found a reasonable probability that the practice it condemned would substantially lessen competition or tend to create a monopoly; but the circumstances probably would not have supported a proceeding under the Sherman Act.

For the present purpose, these thirteen cases need only brief mention. In one case, in 1920, a petroleum company was ordered to cease leasing pumps and tanks below cost to dealers on condition that only its own products be sold.[1] In one case a large company was ordered to divest itself of stock it had acquired in a competing corporation. In one case a company was enjoined from

---

[1] In six parallel cases involving other companies among the leading fifty, the conviction was reversed by the courts, but this company did not appeal.

continuing to operate a subsidiary as a bogus independent. In five cases, three of which involved rubber products, a big company was ordered to cease discriminating in price among its customers; and three more such cases were pending as to gasoline. In two cases, payment of brokerage by a seller to a buyer or a buyer's representative was the offense. Though the competition endangered in the discrimination cases was typically that among buyers, not among the discriminating sellers, two of these cases were directly relevant to the power of the big. In one, the recipitant of allowances equivalent to brokerage was Atlantic & Pacific Tea Co. In the other, General Motors was found not only to have discriminated in the price of spark plugs but also to have used rebates to induce buyers to accept exclusive dealing arrangements.

In 28 cases, the issues raised by the Commission were undistinguishable from those raised under the Sherman Act. They had to do with conspiracy and coercion. The conspiracy cases were most numerous in the steel, rubber, and electrical manufacturing industries. In 1951 all seven of the big steel companies accepted an order terminating a case that charged conspiracy to fix the prices of substantially all of the industry's products by use of a basing point system. Some of these companies were involved in five other conspiracy cases—Republic four times, U. S. Steel, Jones & Laughlin, and Youngstown twice, Bethlehem once. Three of the cases, covering rigid steel conduit, steel drums, and metal rain goods,[1] were concerned with price fixing. General Electric, too, participated in the first of them. In the fourth case, manufacturers of tin plate agreed to cease selling second quality plate as such and instead to require their customers to accept up to 25 percent of such plate in deliveries of first quality. The fifth case, not yet decided, charges that U. S. Steel participated in a plan to

---

[1] Funnels, elbows, etc.

create a monopolistic marketing channel for steel scrap and that for this purpose it used exclusive dealing arrangements and put pressure upon fabricators and railroads.

In the rubber manufacturing industry, four conspiracy cases involved Goodyear and U. S. Rubber, each three times. Three of the cases were concerned with price fixing upon mechanical rubber goods, rubber heels and soles, and power cable and rubber-covered building wire. General Electric participated in the latter conspiracy. The fourth case involved an effort to cut off sales to mail order houses by a reciprocal exclusive dealing arrangement between an association of makers of bicycle parts and an association of jobbers. General Motors participated in this scheme.

In the electrical manufacturing industry, General Electric, besides taking part in the power cable and rigid steel conduit conspiracies already discussed, participated with Westinghouse in a price fixing agreement upon turbine generators.

The remaining conspiracy cases include a price fixing plan for agricultural insecticides and a plan to control the channels for distribution of surgical instruments, in both of which duPont participated; a scheme to fix the prices of lead pigments, to which Anaconda was a party; a price fixing agreement upon paper, involving International Paper; two plans to fix liquor prices, in each of which Schenley participated; use of a jointly owned buying agency by the Standard Oil companies of New Jersey, Indiana, and California (with two other oil companies also participating) to obtain discriminatory prices upon tires, batteries, and automobile parts and accessories; a price fixing arrangement for gasoline in the Tampa, Florida, marketing area, in which Gulf and Texas cooperated; and a price fixing program by wholesale tobacco dealers, which American Tobacco supported by refusing to sell to price cutters.

The cases of coercion and related monopolistic practices found by the Commission also have a Sherman Act flavor. In three instances—one involving photographic film and two involving liquor—the Commission ordered big companies to cease fixing resale prices under circumstances not covered by the exemptions included in the law.[1] A subsidiary of National Dairy Products was ordered to cease obtaining advantages in buying by dominating an association of milk producers. Eastman was found to have bought laboratories suited to the development of motion picture film and, by threatening to enter that business, to have forced a developers' association to agree not to buy foreign film. General Motors was found to have coerced dealers to stock only the parts and accessories which it distributed and to accept shipments they had not ordered. In a pending case, National Dairy Products is accused of supplying fixtures, facilities, services, and even loans at less than cost provided the recipient retail dealers cease to carry any products bought from competitors.

If the Commission's 28 cases of Sherman Act quality are added to the cases presented by the Department of Justice, the composite constitutes 102 cases that have been decided and 12 that are pending. Of the fifty largest industrial companies, all but five have lost one or more such cases, and three of the five are defendants in the pending cases. Only Atlantic Refining and Woolworth have spotless records.

Although the 102 decided cases differ in importance, most of them have been concerned with offenses central to the competitive policy—price fixing, restriction of production, allocation of markets, exclusion of small firms from the industry, coercion of nominally independent enterprises. In most of the cases the power of a big company was reinforced by conspiracy, sometimes

---

[1] Eastman was found to be fixing resale prices on film which was not in competition with other film of like grade and quality, whereas the exemption applies only where there is such competition. Schenley and Seagram were found to be fixing resale prices in the District of Columbia, where there is no resale price exemption.

with other big companies, sometimes with small ones. Even where a monopoly was attained, it was often based upon an agreement with other big companies to allocate territories and industrial fields.

This analysis supports the conclusion that violation of the central prohibitions of the anti-trust laws is too common among big companies to be disregarded or treated as an unimportant aspect of the conduct of these companies. Abuse of power for monopolistic purposes is a significant and recurrent pattern of big business.[1]

---

[1] Since the power derived from sheer bigness is not subject to legal action except when it can be interpreted as a manifestation of monopoly or of monopolistic purpose, no similar list of cases can be used to show precisely the impact of bigness upon competition. The government receives many complaints by small enterprises against large ones, but where the anti-trust laws do not apply most of these remain uninvestigated. Abuses that cause so much stir are probably frequent and substantial; but how much so cannot be shown.

CHAPTER III

THE CASE FOR BIG BUSINESS

The last chapter described the types of power enjoyed by big business and summarized the evidence that such power is often used to weaken or destroy competition. This chapter will describe the competitive influences that bear upon big business and will attempt to evaluate the claims that large enterprises usually follow policies that have been shaped by competition and are beneficial to the public. As the last chapter was concerned with the case against big business, this chapter will be concerned with the case for big business.

Since possession of excessive power and arbitrary abuse of it are frequently investigated and prosecuted, the case against big business rests largely upon detailed charges by public officials, supported by proof. Unfounded accusations cannot be proved, and therefore drop out of the case. Unfortunately, the case for big business is neither equally detailed nor equally authoritative. When business men are believed to be competing fairly and vigorously, they are not investigated and proof in support of the belief is not provided. The claims on their behalf usually rest upon the opinions of observers who do not have access to all the relevant facts and upon the self-serving and therefore unconvincing assertions of officials of large business enterprises. Thus the arguments on behalf of big business may include exaggeration and unfounded praise.

Because of this difference in the origins of the claims and charges, the procedure of this chapter must differ from that of the last. In most of the discussion of abuses it was sufficient to summarize what the government had proved; in discussing alleged virtues, it is necessary to ascertain, so far as paucity of evidence permits, the degree of truth in the allegations. The statement of pros and cons must appear to be biased, because one side of the argument is presented with few qualifications and the other with many. But the nature of the available information makes this disparity inevitable.

The case for big business is hard to summarize because it includes two substantially different lines of argument. Along one line, the standard of competition is accepted, and the acts and policies of big business are cited as evidence that among the big there is adequate competition. Along a second line, the activities of big companies are described as beneficial, usually without specific consideration whether they are competitive, and sometimes with tacit or even explicit admission that they are not. So far as the case for big business rests upon the first type of argument, the critics and defenders of large enterprises accept a common principle and disagree as to the bearing of the facts upon it. So far as the case for big business rests upon defense of what is not competitive, the disagreement extends to principle as well as to facts.

As was indicated in Chapter I, the appropriate question concerns the competitiveness of big business rather than its economic performance. The policy of competition rests upon political as well as economic considerations; and though exceptions to it can be made (with appropriate public regulation) where good economic results can thus be achieved, an exception broad enough to exempt big business as a whole would undermine the political basis of the policy.

But even if the desirability of competition were to be determined solely by economic considerations, there would be difficulties in testing a blanket claim that anti-competitive activities by big business are desirable. When such a claim is made as to the activities of a particular company in a particular market, the trend of events in surrounding markets that are competitive provides a standard for judgment. Prices, profits, and technical progress under competition can be compared with their counterparts under monopoly. Though such comparisons are difficult because of differences between industries and companies, they are not wholly impossible. But claims made on behalf of noncompetitive policies followed by the entire big business community cannot be founded upon such comparisons. It may be possible to show that large enterprises have reduced prices, improved products, expanded productive capacity, and reduced profits. But no outside observer knows whether what has been done in these respects is all that was possible. Even the managements of the big companies do not know how their potential and their performance might have changed under more competitive pressure. Proof that power has not been abused and opportunities have not been lost requires something more than evidence that in a changing world a powerful concern has expanded its output, or incorporated some new technology in its products and processes, or found that lower prices were more profitable, or found that it could no longer obtain its former rate of profit.

Moreover, though a part of the economic argument for competition is based upon the pressures and incentives provided by it moment by moment, much of the argument rests upon the longrun desirability of letting new enterprises try ideas that are thought to be crazy and upon the usefulness of flexible and impersonal response to the changing forces of the economy in such matters as the allocation of resources among occupations. Whether or not a non-competitive system of big business harms the economy as to such matters cannot be ascertained by examining the policies of the various large enterprises.

Though these weaknesses inhere in the argument that big business serves the public and therefore need not be required to compete, this argument is so often made that it cannot be disregarded if the case for big business it to be fairly presented. Accordingly, the discussion that follows will consider not only the influences promoting competition, and the extent to which they make big business competitive, but also the impact of the policies of large enterprises upon the performance of the economy.

Forces That Foster Competition

The first point in the case for the big is that big business is exposed to great forces and pressures that tend to foster competition rather than monopoly. The performance of large business enterprises must be responsive to the major influences of the environment, and these influences are hostile to the steady accumulation and exercise of power by particular enterprises. The era of big business has been one of dynamic change. In one lifetime there have been two world wars, an unprecedentedly severe depression, and two remarkable post-war booms. Even in a fully monopolized economy, these catastrophic changes would have prevented stagnation by forcing business enterprises, large and small, to adapt themselves from time to time to a different environment.

Moreover, there are sustained trends of change, only partly ecnomic in origin, to which business must inevitably accommodate itself. One is the growth of population, which, since 1900, has more than doubled the number of people in the continental United States. A second is the change in the location of these people. In two centuries we have settled a continent and urbanized and then suburbanized our society; and the latest census figures show that great shifts of people are still going on. A third is the rapid growth of scientific knowledge, which has made available a constantly evolving array of technological possibilities.

Such changes are not subject to business control. Though the growth of population is partly the result of more jobs and higher standards of living, it reflects also our changing ways of life and our improving medical skills. Though migrations come partly in response to the changing location of industry, they are produced also by preferences for particular climates and environments. Though business has contributed substantially to scientific progress, major discoveries must be attributed largely to scientists who were not interested in the economic effect of their work. Even the portion of population growth, migration, and scientific development which is properly attributable to business has been the consequence of interacting decisions by many enterprises large and small. To any one business enterprise, even the largest, such trends of change have been uncontrollable forces of the environment.

The impact of these environmental forces has been to reduce the importance and relevance of vested interests acquired in the past, to increase the importance of quick response to what is new, and to inject the continuous stimulus of expansion. Existing accumulations of power have been subjected to attrition. New opportunities to accumulate power have been numerous. Responsiveness to the environment rather than firmness of policy has been the means to power. Our concept of monopoly, derived from a time and place in which environmental changes were less important, emphasizes the effect of monopolistic power in fostering lethargy and repression of new ideas and methods. But in a changing environment such as ours, great power can be retained only if its exercise is not lethargic and only if the powerful concern is at least as swift as others in adapting itself to great social changes. A changing environment, in other words, is a competitive force in that it makes power relatively insecure. The breadth and complexity of the American economy have been such that many promising monopolistic ventures have failed because of a dynamic technology that reshuffled the boundaries of industry, or a dynamic distributive system that opened up new market channels, or a dynamic transportation system that brought in distant competitors, or some other dynamic influence not provided for in the plans of the monopolists.

Another influence toward competition has been the fact that the big enterprises which furnish about half of our manufacturing output must operate in a setting of competition. Large segments of the economy—the major part of distribution and of the service trades, a considerable part of manufacturing and of construction—are basically competitive and are organized in small business units that make competition almost inevitable.[1] So long as such parts of the economy are competitive, the economy as a whole will be broadly competitive as to problems of allocation of resources. The big business segment, whether or not competitive within itself, will be exposed to substantial competition for labor, for investment funds, and for such materials as cannot be preemptively monopolized. The competitive elements in the big business segment will be strengthened, the monopolistic elements weakened. Moreover, the competitive parts of the economy do much to keep business ideology focussed upon competition, so that the pursuit of monopolistic power by any business must be disavowed even in talking to other business men.

Our governmental policy of maintaining competition is strengthened by this favorable climate of business opinion and in turn does much to keep both business opinion and the underlying business relationships competitive. In spite of minor variations, this policy has been pursued with remarkable consistency for two-thirds of a century. The very existence of the policy encourages big business to be circumspect in acquiring and using power. The anti-trust laws have had a substantial impact upon American business by keeping restrictive agreements illegal and driving them underground, by protecting small business against overt destruction and coercion, by strengthening the backbones

---

[1] Although attempts to restrict competition collusively are common in such areas of small business, they usually break down quickly because of conflicting interests among the participants.

of business enterprises that are independently minded, and by subjecting the monopolist or the would-be monopolist to harassment even in cases where public action to destroy his power is not effective. Thus monopolistic activity in this country has been weaker, riskier, briefer, and more exposed to attack both from Government and from competitive business than it would have been under a different legal system.

The generally competitive environment has tended to drain the strength from particular monopolistic elements therein, and the strongly competitive policy of the country, applied through legal proceedings, has tended, in spite of local failures, to prevent the gains of monopolies from being consolidated and to keep the environment generally competitive.

The most important of the incentives of big business, the desire to grow, often points toward competition. The executives of large concerns share the general American belief that neither an economy, an industry, nor a business enterprise is healthy unless it is becoming larger. For most of them this belief is strengthened by direct personal interest, since the growth of the enterprise they control is likely to bring them personally more power, more prestige, and a larger salary or bonus or gain from stock options. So far as the policies of a big corporation are designed to foster its growth, they tend to discourage some of the worst of the monopolistic vices, such as restriction of output and suppression of new processes and products, and they may easily bring the expanding company into competition with others that also desire to expand.

Nevertheless, the incentive to grow is not a guarantee of competition. An enterprise may grow in six directions:

    (a) by capturing business from a rival;
    (b) by successfully invading an industry in which it was not previously engaged;
    (c) by introducing new products, previously sold by nobody;

(d) by obtaining a portion of the growth of an industry in which it is already engaged;

(e) by absorbing an established business;

(f) by reciprocal allocation of fields of business, so that it automatically benefits from any growth that takes place in the field allocated to it.

The first and second of these possibilities can be attained only by direct competition with rivals, old or new. The third possibility involves no more than an indirect competition of substitutes, the intensity of which is uncertain. Similarly, the fourth possibility may involve competition of varying degrees of intensity or passivity. The fifth possibility does not require competition and may be anti-competitive in tendency. The sixth possibility is the antithesis of competition. Without desire to grow, an enterprise would not undertake the competition that leads to growth; but with desire to grow its methods may be competitive, non-competitive, anti-competitive, or a mixture of the three.

Types of Competition

If environmental pressure and the incentive to grow make big business competitive, the competition must show itself in direct rivalry between particular big companies and other business enterprises. It will be convenient to divide the consideration of the extent of such direct competitive rivalry into three topics: first, competition between big companies and little companies in the same industry; second competition among big companies that are primarily engaged in the same industry; and third, competition among big companies that are primarily engaged in different industries.

The first topic needs only brief discussion. Though the entire mass of little companies may substantially affect the economy-wide allocation of resources, within a single industry competition between the big and the little is seldom an effective curb upon the power of the big nor an effective protection for the consumer. The tendency is for small companies to follow the lead of big ones in selecting a price; and even when a small enterprise sells substantially the same product at a lower price it usually entices so few customers away from its big rival that the latter feels no need to reduce its price to the same level. Moreover, the big concern can discipline small rivals by local price cutting and the other devices noted in the last chapter; and its ability to do so is so evident that it seldom need do more than allow the small concerns to discipline themselves through their own fears. There probably are occasional situations in which the competition of small companies is effective in curbing the activities of enterprises somewhat larger; the competition of the latter is an effective curb upon still larger concerns; and thus, in gradations like stair-steps, a continuous system of checks runs from the smallest to the largest. Probably there are also situations in which a small concern can compete effectively against larger ones because it has strength derived from location, patents, or exceptionally good management. But such instances are not numerous enough to make small business a generaly effective regulator of the power of big business. Where there is a great gap of size between the little and the big, the little enterprises are typically powerless to affect the policies of the big ones.

But one big company can curb another; and a considerable part of the argument that big business and competition are consistent with each other rests upon the belief that the relation between large enterprises in the same industry is adequately competitive. This second topic deserves detailed examination.

Short-Run Price Policies

First, let us note that the competitiveness of big business is never asserted on the basis of the short-run price policies of the big. These are treated as unimportant. There is general agreement that where a few big companies produce most of an industry's product short-run price competition seldom exists.[1] Change in quoted prices is infrequent. Large concerns usually set prices by administrative decisions made infrequently, and are reluctant to adjust prices to take account of day-to-day fluctuations in the market.[2] When they make price concessions to meet momentary pressures, they usually do so in the form of special discounts or secret rebates to particular large customers. Indeed, the impor-

---

[1] The most substantial statistical study of the relation between concentration and inflexibility of prices appears in TNEC Monograph No. 27, *The Structure of Industry,* pp. 340-412. It concludes that no signficant relationship between concentration and price behavior can be demonstrated, but that there is a conspicuous relationship between price behavior and the characteristics of the product, differentiating durable goods from non-durables, consumers' goods from industrial raw materials, etc. However, the study was concerned with certain contemporary controversies about concentration, and, for various reasons, is not directly relevant to the point at issue here. It concerns net price change over a period of several years, not short-run price fluctuations; it concerns net realized prices, that is, the average net receipt from a line of similar goods, not the prices actually quoted or received for the particular items in the line; instead of centering upon the question whether substantial differences in concentration are related to differences in price behavior among products that are similar in most respects, it centers upon the question whether varying degrees of concentration, not all of which are significant, have a traceable effect among groups of unlike products. For other studies of the same subject see Alfred C. Neal, *Industrial Concentration and Price Inflexibility.* (American Council on Public Affairs, 1942) and National Resources Committee, *The Structure of the American Economy, 1939,* Part I, p. 142. A recent study which tends to refute the TNEC Monograph is John Blair, "Economic Concentration and Depression Price Rigidity," *American Economic Review,* May, 1955.

[2] The most conspicuous exceptions to this rule are cases in which the administrative decision has been to keep the price in a fixed relationship to the fluctuating price of a raw material; and in these instances, though the price changes often, the formula by which it is set does not.

tance of discriminatory price concessions as a means to short-run flexibility in prices has become so great that in recent discussions of price discrimination it has often been argued that if special discounts are prevented price competition itself is jeopardized.

The relative rigidity of the prices set by large companies means, of course, that market fluctuations must be met in some other way than by price change. If the device used is the secret special discount, a problem of discrimination is created. If no price concessions are made and the fluctuations of demand are not great, the big company may be able to accept a fluctuating sales volume, offset it with fluctuations in inventories and financial balances, and keep the physical processes of production flowing regularly. So far as this can be done, no important economic loss arises from the inflexibility of day-to-day prices. But if the irregularity of sales is too great to be thus compensated, the effect of price rigidity must be to throw the burden of adjustment on the physical operations of the concern, thus creating wasteful irregularity in mechanized processes and in the employment of human labor.

Some large concerns avoid, not only day-to-day price changes, but also price adjustments to reflect the changing conditions of a business cycle.[1] Certain large enterprises have claimed, and been accorded, public approval because during a boom they have increased prices more slowly and by smaller amounts than market conditions would have permitted. In general, the same enterprises, together with some that have not shown similar forbearance in boom times, have insisted, in the face of public criticism, that price reductions during a depression are a mistake, to be avoided

---

[1] See footnote 1, p. 136 for reference to studies of the relation between such rigidities and concentration. Since the evidence as to the frequency of such a relationship is inconclusive, the point made here is that such rigidity is a pattern that sometimes reflects the policy of the big, but there is no intention to assert that it is the only pattern of big business policy toward prices in depression.

if possible. An example of this point of view is to be found in the testimony of Benjamin Fairless of U.S. Steel in March, 1955.[1] In discussion which followed an inquiry whether there was real competition in the steel industry, Mr. Fairless said,

> "There has been a change in our thinking. Price is not the only form of competition. We also compete by quality and service."

He accepted a suggestion by the questioner that talk about price competition might be unrealistic under our new conditions, and added that with its profit objective in mind U.S. Steel had sometimes decided not to meet lower prices. Senator Fulbright then inquired further,

> "You feel we may have a false idea of the value of price competition as it existed fifty years ago and that the people who long for it may be completely wrong?"

> "Yes." Mr. Fairless replied, "Don't forget that steel prices were very low in the depression years, and that didn't seem to help much, did it?"

So long as business executives are encouraged to keep prices artifically low during a boom, they will feel encouraged to keep prices artifically high during depression. But it is questionable whether during a boom the growth of demand should be stimulated and the pattern of consumption distorted by price patterns that rigidly resist increase. Price rigidity during a recession is even more questionable. In defense of such rigidity, the advocates of big business patterns of pricing often say that price reductions would not do much to increase the volume of business, both because the relevant demand is inelastic and because when prices are falling the crucial basis for reduced demand is lack of confidence. They point out that the most rigid prices of the great depression were those of the capital goods industries, whose pro-

---

[1] *New York Times,* March 22, 1955.

duction could not be sold because the customers saw no chance to use more capital goods at a profit. This argument has point, but does not prove enough. Though lower prices will not stimulate sales as much in a depression as in prosperity, prices that do not fall must stimulate sales still less, particularly in any case in which a disparity is created between the rigid prices and other prices that have fallen. Moreover, the lack of confidence that springs from falling prices and disappearance of profits is not as well founded as the lack of confidence that comes from the vicious spiral of unemployment, inability to buy, reduced demand, and further unemployment. Finally, when a recession passes its low point a revival of demand is likely to appear earlier if prices are low than if they are high. It was not accidental that the final report of the President's Committee of Industrial Analysis upon the operations of the National Recovery Administration concluded that "In general, those industries which were most successful in maintaining prices were least successful in maintaining a satisfactory level of production and development."[1]

Long-Run Price Policies

The long-run price policies of big business, as distinguished from the short-run price policies that have just been discussed, are frequently described as farsightedly competitive. In one sense this cannot be true; for a price that results from the interacting pressures of competition cannot be accurately described as the product of any concern's policy. In a broader sense, however, a price policy may have been established in recognition of competitive

---

[1] National Recovery Administration, *Message from the President of the United States transmitting a report on the operation of the National Recovery Administration which has been prepared by the members of the Committee of Industrial Analysis who have no official relationship to the Government. (House Document 158, 75th Congress, 1st Session;* Washington D. C., Government Printing Office, 1937) pp. 163-164.

pressures and may be intended to serve as a means of competing. It is in this sense that a price policy may or may not express competition.

At their best, the price policies of American big business show a daring and imaginative pursuit of greater sales. In a few notable cases, large enterprises have reduced prices further than their existing costs would permit, relying upon lower prices to enhance their sales and upon increased sales to reduce their costs sufficiently to make the new prices profitable. Conspicuous examples appear in the early history of the Ford Motor Company, though perhaps before the company could properly be called large. Great Atlantic & Pacific Tea Company furnishes a more recent example, though in this case the company's policy had overtones of local price cutting, discrimination, and destruction of competitors that resulted in judicial condemnation.[1] But policies so daring appear to be rare. More frequently a large enterprise is unwilling to take the risk of reducing prices in anticipation of changes in sales and in costs, but reduces prices after existing levels of sales and costs have come to justify the reduction.[2] Though more conservative

---

[1] *U.S. v. New York Great Atlantic & Pacific Tea Co.,* 67 F. Supp. 626, 173 F. (2d) 79.

[2] In reducing prices after costs are lowered, a big company does by policy what a wholly competitive market would force it to do through the pressure of competition. Where costs are lowered and profit margins increased, a competitive industry composed of many small sellers attracts new sellers and evokes expansion by old ones, so that volume grows and prices fall. But a planned price reduction is not an exact equivalent to such a competitive one. In a competitive market prices may drop under competitive pressure even when reductions are not justified by lower costs, and thus concerns may be forced against their will to experiment with the volume-increasing and cost-lowering effects of reduced prices. Only in the rare case in which the big company cuts its prices first and expects the low costs to come afterward is there any equivalent for this competitive phenomenon in a big company's long-run price policy.

than the first policy, this type of pricing can also produce dynamic changes wherever each price cut enlarges operations and lowers costs sufficiently to support a further cut. A considerable part of American big business apparently thinks that large volume and quick turnover are signs of business health, that prices should be set as low as costs permit in order to attain as large a volume as possible, and that cost reduction should be one of the chief preoccupations of management. This belief contrasts sharply with the prevailing opinion in certain other countries where it is taken for granted by business men that one should buy cheap and sell dear without exploring the potentialities of increased volume, and that no price should be reduced if a reduction can be avoided.

One cannot safely assume that every instance in which prices are repeatedly cut to enhance volume is an instance of price competition. A record of price reduction and expansion may reflect farsighted competition, but alternatively it may reflect a belated and partial adaption to circumstances that, had there been more competition, would have evoked faster and more far-reaching price cuts. Even a complete monopoly, eager to exploit its power to the limit, will set a price low enough to produce the most profitable volume of sales and may reduce that price from time to time in recognition of changes in demand or cost. A record of price reductions suggests but does not prove the existence of price competition and suggests but does not prove that the economic performance of the concern has been good.

But unfortunatly the policy of low prices, though common in American big business, is not universal there. There are frequent instances of a second price policy, which conforms to the pattern that economists have attributed to oligopoly: Each concern avoids price reductions in the belief that its rivals would follow and that with prices generally lower the volume of business would increase too little to offset the drop in the profit margin. In the years before the second world war one firm of management engineers sought to win converts to this view by arguing that a price reduction to hold one's proportion of an industry's sales was justifiable, but that a price reduction to increase that proportion at the expense of other enterprises invited retaliation and thus assured loss of profits by all.

There are also instances of a third type of price policy, in which a large company keeps prices high and thereby avoids subjecting smaller and weaker concerns to competitive pressure. In such cases the large company sometimes appears to regard its forbearance as a virtue, on the assumption, first, that by competition the weaker rivals would be destroyed rather than forced to strengthen themselves, and second, that the objective of the policy of competition is to preserve competitors rather than to subject a market to competitive pressures. In the period since the second world war, there have been repeated assertions in industry gossip that General Motors could reduce the price of automobiles by as much as $100, but has refrained from doing so lest it destroy other automobile companies. The facts, of course, are not available to the public.

There is also a fourth type of long-run policy. This is the deliberate maintenance of a high price in the belief that demand is so inelastic that lower prices would be less profitable. A striking instance is the price of tungsten carbide, which had been $50 per pound until General Electric obtained exclusive rights to the American market, but thereafter varied between $215 and $450 per pound.[1] Though prices so exhorbitant are fortunately rare, the prevalence of the exploitative type of policy is attested by the frequency with which the largest corporations have been succssfully prosecuted for taking part in a price-fixing conspiracy.

---

[1] Patents, *Hearings Before the Committee on Patents,* U.S. Senate, 77th Congress, 2d Session, (Washington, Government Printing Office, 1942) Part I, pp. 38-520, especially pp. 85-86.

A fifth type of long-run price policy is also encountered. It consists in adopting high-price and low-price policies simultaneously or consecutively. Where high and low prices are used simultaneously, a product is deliberately differentiated to afford a basis for charging a high price where it can be obtained and a low price where no more would be paid. Where high and low price policies are used consecutively, the development of a mass market at a low price may be deliberately delayed until the seller has made the limited sales that are possible at luxury prices. The early history of electric refrigerators provides an illustration of both types of price differentiation. The cream of the luxury market was first skimmed. Then the largest manufacturers began to offer a large box at a luxury price and a small box at a price designed for mass marketing, even though there was a negligible difference in cost between the large box and the small one. This policy persisted until a mail order house, a newcomer in the industry, broke it by offering a large box at a mass production price.

In some instances there are two stages in the price policy of a large company, that in which the market is being created and that in which it is being exploited. The Aluminum Company, for example, reduced the price of aluminum ingot from a level appropriate for jewelry to about 20 cents per pound during the period in which the market for the metal was being developed. Over a quarter of a century later, at the beginning of the second world war, the price was again 20 cents per pound, in spite of the fact that many economies in aluminum manufacture had been achieved in the interval. But when an anti-trust proceeding put pressure upon the company, the price was reduced to fifteen cents per pound, even in the face of a war-time boom in demand.[1] Similarly, during the development of the automobile the price

---

[1] Charlotte F. Muller, *Light Metals Monopoly*, (New York, Columbia University Press, 1946) especially pp. 195-6, 239.

was progressively reduced until the cheapest models sold for less than $300. But sometime in the 1920's the industry's emphasis shifted from cheapness to quality,[2] so that from year to year the mass-produced cars of today show an improvement in performance rather than a price reduction.

The long-run price policies of big business, at their best, provide approximately the results to be expected from competition. However, several other varieties of long-run price policy are also visible, and these express a live-and-let-live avoidance of competition or an exploitative use of power. An estimate of the relative prevalence of the various types of policy must rest upon impressions rather than evidence. But granted the impression that price-reducing policies are more common than price maintaining ones and that the former are usually competitive, the latter are, nevertheless, too important to be disregarded. Blanket approval of the price policies of big business would be as rash as blanket condemnation. The appropriate attitude appears to be one of selective surveillance.

Product Improvement and Development

The aspect of big business policy that is most commonly offered for praise is the improvement of old products and the development of new ones. We are told that the competition of the big has shifted from price to quality.

If this is true, it is not an adequate excuse for any impairment of price competition for which big business may be responsible. Quality competition and price competition are both needed in a healthy economy. They serve different purposes. Quality competition at a given level of price may give the buyer who can afford

---

[2] For a contemporary record of the change see Lawrence H. Seltzer, *A Financial History of the American Automobile Industry,* (Boston, Houghton Mifflin Co., 1928) pp. 59-63, 120-23.

the price a better product; but it does not thereby create new possibilities of sale to persons who cannot pay so much. Competition that fully protects the buyer must furnish acceptable goods at low prices as well as better goods at higher prices.

But quality competition is important in itself; and if big business is competitive in this regard, the point should be emphasized. We are told that the competition of big companies is largely responsible for the reliability of what we buy and for the innovations that have raised our standard of living.

There is a great deal of truth in this. In the products of big companies there is less unplanned variation and hence less unreliability than in the products of most small companies. Since mass production promotes uniformity of product, the big company's ability to push the techniques of mass production further than the small company makes uniformity of product easier for the big company. Moreover, national brand advertising is undertaken only by companies big enough to afford it; and in general, where considerable amounts of money are invested to identify a product in the consumer's mind, the seller's care for his investment requires him to make the product uniform and to rid it of such objectionable characteristics as the buyer can readily perceive. Only the itinerant peddler who will be gone before he is found out can afford to sell his customer a wooden nutmeg.

But one cannot safely assume that the consumer's preference for the products of big companies can be explained solely by the superiority of those products nor that competitive efforts by the big to win favor consist solely in actual improvement of quality.

Merchandising by many large companies has come to rely upon the arts of mass persuasion. The big enterprise no longer sells the consumer merely what he wants. Rather, it does much to persuade him to want what it chooses to make. At its best, mass persuasion channels the tastes of consumers in such a way as to eliminate much of the desire for non-functional ornamentation and for meaningless diversity and thereby to make possible a wider use of standard goods cheaply and efficiently produced by machine processes. But mass persuasion also weakens the capacity of the consumer to resist useless diversity in the characteristics of products and useless changes in those characteristics. Some large producers take advantage of this weakness by differentiating products in functionally meaningless ways as a mere excuse for price difference. Some large producers also introduce meaningless differences from year to year, as in the case of many of the style changes in the bodies of automobiles, in order to hasten the obsolescence of what has already been bought. With the growth of synthetic substances and the disappearance of handicraft techniques of production, the increasing ignorance of the consumer about the composition of the products he uses forces him to rely more and more on what he is told by the seller, and the increasing use of psychological and even psychiatric studies by large sellers makes their persuasive selling increasingly adept in pulling the emotional triggers that lead to action. The consumer is not a mere creature of the advertiser, but neither is he completely in control of his own preferences. Hence his acceptance of the products which he is offered cannot safely be regarded as evidence that these products always deserve dispassionate commendation. The competition of big advertisers for the consumer's patronage must be regarded as a mixture of effort to serve him and effort to manipulate him.

There is also a great deal of truth in the statement that big companies have been the source of new technology and thus of new products and processes. When this claim is made in a way that denies the contributions of the non-commercial scientist, the individual inventor, and the small enterprise, it must be rejected; for many new discoveries, new products, and even new industries have begun in the work of small companies and unattached individuals. But research and development by a great corporation makes it own substantial contribution to technological progress. The big corporation assembles facilities that are too expensive for the small company or the individual. It can undertake systematic exploration of the variables in an unknown field, which would not be possible for an enterprise with a research staff too small for coordinated effort. It can pool the risks and costs of different experiments, of which some are likely to be profitable; whereas a small concern, unable to determine which experiments were promising, could not afford the chance of loss. It can spend larger sums than a small concern for development of a new field and wait longer for operation therein to become profitable. Thus it can explore certain technological frontiers that are not open to the small. The results of such work are presented to us constantly under the brands of the big companies. The rivalry of these companies in research and development is a significant instance of competition.

But not all big companies are technological leaders. Alongside the pattern of the chemical industry, which centers upon research and product development, stands the pattern of the steel industry, in which the biggest concern has been laggard in adopting such improvements as the continuous strip mill and continuous casting. Outstanding performance in improving products is one, but only one, of the patterns of bigness.

Moreover, where research is a central interest, the big company's control of new technology does not rest solely upon research. In many lines of activity neither the individual inventor nor the small company controlling an invention has the resources to exploit the invention commercially. Capital, market connections, or access to other patented technology may be lacking. Thus the invention must remain unused or be sold, often to a big company which controls related patents. By buying inventions, a big company usually acquires patent control of considerably more of the new technology than it has originated. Thus its leadership in innovation is partly derived from its financial power.

Though research by big companies is usually competitive, exploitation of the patents that result from research, as was indicated in Chapter II, frequently is not so.[1] By acquiring many patents, each large company attains control over an assortment of bits of technology and often finds that some of the bits that it needs to use are controlled by others. In a few instances—among them, the automobile industry—patent rights are exchanged, without restrictions, so that all the available methods become the basis of technological competition.[2] More frequently, however, a large corporate patent owner resorts to one of two other policies. On the one hand, it may withhold its patents from use by others (even when they cover processes it does not intend to use) and may thus attempt to block the technological development of rival concerns.[3] Though such a policy is in one sense competitive, it is, in another sense, a predatory exercise of market power. On the other hand, the large patent-owner may exchange patents with its rivals on the explicit condition that commercial competition in using the patents shall be sharply restricted. In the extreme case, each party to the exchange may undertake to use the patents only in a field from which the other parties have agreed to abstain. Thus competition in research may become the basis for collusion in marketing.[4]

Like the mixed record as to price policy, this mixed record as to quality competition and innovation cannot be summarized in one sweeping appraisal. There is much in it that is vigorously competitive and obviously useful; but some of it involves anti-

---

[1] See above, pp. 59-62.

[2] *Investigation of the Concentration of Economic Power, Hearings before the Temporary National Economic Committee,* 75th Congress, 3d Session, (Washington, Government Printing Office, 1939) pp. 253-376.

[3] *Ibid,* pp. 387-396.

[4] *U.S. v. Imperial Chemical Industries, Ltd., et al.,* 105 F. Supp. 215.

competitive abuses of power. No evidence is available to show what proportion of the expenditures of big companies upon research, product design, and sales effort is devoted to rivalry in the introduction of improved products and what proportion to a perverted and manipulative competition or to the consolidation and exploitation of concentrated power. The competitive and the anti-competitive aspects are both too important to be ignored.

Efficiency of Operation

Big business is often praised for its relative efficiency. We are told that big companies have low costs and that this fact is a principal source of their power. Such assertions imply that the big compete with one another and with the little as to efficiency, that an efficient small company has nothing to fear, and that the victory of the efficient big is good for the economy.

Doubtless big companies, like little ones, try to be efficient. Efforts to cut costs are pervasive in our economy. Since the end of the war comments of visiting foreign business men have indicated that the intensity of this effort among American large enterprises is exceptional by European standards and that the greater competitiveness of American business accounts for much of the difference.[1]

But the claim that big business in this country is more efficient than small rests upon mere assertion. Various efforts have been made to study statistically the relative efficiency of producers of different size. The results have been inconclusive, primarily because the available data were scattered, not directly comparable, and of doubtful relevance.[2] In the absence of reliable data, the

[1] See for example, Anglo-American Council on Productivity, *Productivity Team Report—Steel Founding,* (London, September, 1949); *Productivity Report, Industrial Engineering,* (September, 1954).

[2] See Richards C. Osborn, *Effects of Corporate Size on Efficiency and Profitability,* (Urbana, Illinois, University of Illinois Bureau of Economic and Business Research, Bulletin Series No. 72, 1950).

relative efficiency of large and small companies cannot be demonstrated merely by their relative success in the industries that contain both; for big companies may prosper because of power such as was discussed in the last chapter; small companies may occupy crannies of the industry, too small for big companies to invade; and small companies may prosper under the protective umbrella of the big.

In the absence of satisfactory evidence, we are thrown back upon theory. Bigness logically permits functional specialization of management, the development of specialized service departments, and a ready cross-fertilization of ideas among specialized persons. It also permits heavy lump-sum expenditures for equipment, research, advertising, or any other purpose, because their cost can be spread thinly over many units of output. These are elements of efficiency. They may be reinforced by internal competition among the managers of duplicate units; and such competition, measured by a uniform accounting standard, may focus upon efficiency more sharply than competition in the market. On the other hand, bigness logically creates a gap between top management and operations, necessitates costly information services and chains of command to bridge the gap, and requires policy decisions to establish coherence among subordinates. Where information is insufficient, decisions are likely to be bad. Chains of command readily produce red-tape and buck-passing. Policy directives readily produce inflexibility. Rivalries within the concern and failures of control from above readily produce intrigue and operation at cross purposes. These are elements of inefficiency. While such elements are easy to catalog, the relative importance of the various aspects cannot be determined by logic. Moreover, it probably varies greatly from case to case.[1]

---

[1] Cf. Eliot Jones, *The Trust Problem in the United States,* (New York, Macmillan, 1929) Chapter 19.

From common knowledge, it is apparent that the efficiency of big companies differs greatly from company to company. Certain great concerns, such as duPont and General Motors, appear to explore techniques of production systematically and to have used great skill in developing techniques of management. The desire to imitate their methods and to hire their personnel appears to be common enough that one can hardly doubt their efficiency. On the other hand, gross inefficiency apparently does not destroy the power of big companies. A recent crisis of inefficiency in the Ford Motor Company led to drastic reorganization.[1] About twenty years ago United States Steel Corporation was severely criticized for inefficiency by a firm of consulting engineers that had been hired to make recommendations for improvement. Though the report of these engineers has never been made public, testimony concerning that report in congressional hearings indicates that defects of organization and of performance were numerous and considerable.[2]

In considering the alleged efficiency of big companies, one should be careful to distinguish between true efficiency and the power to reduce costs by transferring burdens to weaker business enterprises. If a company is big enough to have great bargaining power, it may be able, as was shown in Chapter II, to buy its raw materials at exceptionally low prices, and this buying advantage may be a major source of lower costs. Some discriminatory advantages are obtained only by violating or evading the law against price discrimination. But in the purchase of raw materials and components a big manufacturer may obtain discounts that are not forbidden by law. The Federal Trade Commission found, for example, that spark plugs were sold to large automobile com-

---

[1] Ford Motor Co., *Ford at Fifty, 1903-1953,* (New York, Simon and Schuster, 1953) pp. 86-87.

[2] *Investigation of Concentration of Economic Power, op. cit.,* Part 4A, pp. 589, 624-628; 644-649, 966-972.

panies as equipment for new cars at prices that probably were below cost, while the makers of the plugs obtained higher prices from smaller manufacturers and made most of their profits from replacement sales. The buying advantage of the large automobile manufacturer in purchase for original equipment was not found to be forbidden by law.[1]

But the advantage of the big company may reach beyond a mere difference in buying prices. One aspect of the efficiency of large automobile manufacturers which has often been praised is the speed with which the raw material inventories are put to use and the close dove-tailing between purchase of materials and manufacture of cars which minimizes the need for inventories. This element of efficiency appeared in a new light when the NRA Advisory Council examined a petition from upholstery manufacturers who wanted their code relaxed so that their productive operations could be less regular. The reason given for the request was that in selling to the automobile industry a maker of upholstery must be prepared to change rates of delivery by large percentages upon short notice and that the irregularity of purchases by the automobile makers subjected him to inescapable irregularity of production. Efficiency in automobile upholstery buying and inefficiency in the production of automobile upholstery were apparently two aspects of the same process, one in which certain costs of the irregularities of production were shifted from the automobile industry to the upholstery industry.[2]

---

[1] *In the Matter of General Motors Corporation and A C Spark Plug Co.*, Federal Trade Commission Docket No. 5620, Findings as to the Facts and Conclusion, July 10, 1953. *In the Matter of Champion Spark Plug Company*, FTC Docket 3977, Finding as to the Facts and Conclusion, July 10, 1953. *In the Matter of Electric Auto-Lite Co.*, FTC Docket 5624, Findings as to the Facts and Conclusion, July 10, 1953.

[2] *NRA Advisory Council Decisions*, Vol. III, pp. 250-255 (mimeographed, undated.)

In a large business enterprise elements of true efficiency and elements of bargaining power that masquerade as efficiency are intermingled. Even with full access to the facts it would be hard to disentangle the two. With a smattering of facts, it is impossible. The claim that big business enterprises compete for efficiency may be accepted. The claim that they tend to be more efficient than smaller concerns must be regarded as not proven.

Inter-industry Competition

In the case for big business, an increasing amount of emphasis has been placed upon competition among big companies in different industries. We are told that the large producers in any one industry are exposed to competition by large producers in other industries. This competition takes two forms: First, a commodity that is an appropriate part of one industry's product-mix may be found useful for purposes that have been traditionally served by the products of another industry. Thus arises competition among substitutes—orlon with wool or cotton, nylon with silk, aluminum with copper, plastics with aluminum. Second, a concern primarily engaged in one industry may add to its line of products certain ones that fall within another industry. Thus arises inter-industrial diversification—Anaconda Company begins to produce aluminum or General Motors to produce deisel engines. By either means, we are told, concentration of control over production in a single industry is made unimportant by competition across industry lines.

There can be no doubt that the competition of substitutes and inter-industrial diversification have eroded the power of some big companies and that such possibilities are an important part of the competitive potential. But they are not important enough to replace all other kinds of competition. Though some substitutes replace each other adequately, so that each is fully exposed to competition from the other, there are many substitutes which will be accepted only with reluctance; and in such instances the availability of the substitute can limit monopoly power but cannot destroy it. The complexity of such relationships was apparent in the cellophane case,[1] in which the lower court acquitted duPont because of inter-product competition. The record showed that duPont sold about 76 percent of all cellophane in the United States and that the remainder was produced under duPont patents by a licensee restricted to a fixed percentage of duPont's sales. The court held, however, that other flexible wrapping materials, (paper, films, and foils of various kinds) competed with cellophane so intensely that "acquisition of market control or monopoly power is a practical impossibility." This conclusion was supported by evidence, persuasive to the court, that duPont behaved like a competitor by conducting research to improve quality and reduce cost, by promoting the development and use of packaging machinery, by providing technical services as to the use of cellophane, by making studies of markets and buying habits, by persuasive selling, and by price reduction.

An array of problems will confront the Supreme Court in deciding the Government's appeal in this case. The various substitute wrapping materials differ from cellophane in respects that are important to different degrees in wrapping different products —resistence to moisture, grease, and heat, transparency, limpness, ease of printing, bursting strength, and tearing strength. The prices of these substitutes range from less than one third to nearly three times the price of cellophane, and these ratios change substantially from time to time because the various prices do not move together. The proportion of total sales obtained by cellophane varies widely; for bakery products it was less than 7 percent in 1949, whereas for cigarettes it is 100 percent whenever adequate supplies are available. Neither identity of prices nor

---

[1] *U.S. v. E. I. duPont de Nemours & Co.,* 118 F. Supp. 41,

stable price ratios nor price competition appear to be forced upon the various producers by their rivalry with one another.[1] In the light of such considerations and of duPont's policies, the court must decide whether inter-product competition is strong enough to overcome evidence that the particular product cellophane is restrictively controlled.

But even if different degrees of substitutability created no problem, we could not rely wholly upon inter-product and inter-industry competition. For many important commodities, such as the automobile tire, there is no satisfactory substitute. Where diversified companies are established in various industries, substitutes are sometimes under a single corporate control. Agreements between producers of the substitutes sometimes prevent effective competition. Agreements to allocate fields sometimes prevent or limit diversification in the direction in which competition is needed. Thus, in particular cases, the competition between industries is seriously limited; and since the arrangements that limit it are often secret, the extent of the limitation remains largely unknown.

Because of inter-industry competition, big business is more competitive than it appears. Because of limits imposed upon inter-industry competition by ownership and agreement, big business is less competitive than such competition could make it. Because of the inherent limits of inter-industry competition, it alone cannot provide an adequate amount of competition among large enterprises.

Defenses of Big Business in The Light of The Evidence

In the light of this quick survey of the principal types of competitive pressure to which large enterprises are exposed, let

---

[1] For a summary and analysis of the facts, see George W. Stocking, and Willard F. Mueller, "The Cellophane Case and the New Competition," *American Economic Review,* March 1955, pp. 29-63.

us consider again the five types of rationale for big business which were summarized in Chapter I.

First, we are told that the economy behaves like a competitive one in growth, technical progress, and rising standards of living. To base such an argument upon our post-war prosperity is over-optimistic. The post-war boom of the late 1940's and early 1950's contrasts sharply with the industrial lethargy of the 1930's. There is a possibility that just as some of us then misread the depression as a full expression of the basic forces of the economy, so some of us are today interpreting a boom largely due to defense expenditures as evidence of enduring health and of the competition which we believe produces health. But a longer trend supports the conclusion also. Over the last half century, industries in which big business is important have shown a substantial increase in the quality of products, a substantial decline in the cost of producing many types of commodities, a substantial decline in the prices of these commodities, and a substantial increase in amounts produced. Concerns that have pioneered in price cutting and cost reduction have grown and become leaders in important fields of business activity. Many new enterprises have appeared, and the relative size and strength of existing enterprises has changed substantially from decade to decade. New products have taken the place of old products; new processes have replaced old processes; and new channels of distribution have established themselves alongside old ones. The big business world has not been frozen in the model of its vested interests. Instead it has shown the flexibility and change characteristic of competition and has moved in the direction of reducing prices and costs and maximizing sales, as the theorists tell us that a competitive system is likely to do.

But the dynamic growth of the economy is attributable in large part to forces for which neither big business nor competition is responsible — population growth, migration, the cumulative growth of scientific knowledge, and perhaps also the disrupting effect of two great wars. Such forces tend to weaken monopolistic vested interests and thus preserve competition. They probably make big business more competitive than it would otherwise be. But their existence and the changes for which they are responsible do not demonstrate that big business is adequately competitive. Our rate of economic progress may be promoted by the competitiveness of large enterprises or retarded by their lack of competitiveness. The mere fact that we do advance is not sufficient to prove either hypothesis.

Second, the creative destruction emphasized by Professor Schumpeter is one important element in the behavior of large business enterprises, and is often a highly competitive element. But such technological competition is not a sufficient substitute for all other forms of competition. Some purposes are served by price competition that cannot be served by the introduction of new products and processes, even if such innovations are made at low prices. Moreover, although it is obvious that expensive research can be undertaken only by those who can undertake the expense, vigorous technological innovation is not characteristic of all large businesses; and some that do emphasize it have used it, not to compete, but to pool patents in agreements designed to restrict competition. Furthermore, small companies as well as large take part in this process of creative destruction. The automobile assembly line began as an innovation by a mechanic in a small-town shed. The electric light, the telephone, and the airplane were invented by individuals who had no large organization behind them. Minute-Maid, Tracerlab and a host of other companies are demonstrating that today innovation is not confined to industrial giants. No one can say how much of our technical progress would stop if we were forced to rely upon small companies only. How much Professor Schumpeter's argument should be discounted is anybody's guess, but there is considerable evidence that an appreciable discount is needed.

Third, the countervailing power stressed by Professor Galbraith as a system of checks and balances alternative to competition does curb the power of some large companies in some circumstances. Government has curbed the market policies of the large enterprises, by anti-trust proceedings and otherwise; unions have modified the labor policies of the big employer as well as the small; and big buyers have been able to obtain special discounts and other favors, even from big sellers. But such checks and balances do not mesh very well. Concessions obtained by large buyers tend to be discriminatory and not to protect small buyers. The biggest manufacturers tend to sell to small distributors, the biggest distributors to buy from small manufacturers.[1] When the big deal with the little, countervailing power is at a minimum. Moreover, the compromise between powerful antagonists does not necessarily protect the interests of third parties: a big union and a big company may agree upon a wage increase for which funds are to be provided by a price increase unwelcome to small consumers who have no adequate countervailing power. Thus countervailing power is an insufficient principle to assure a balanced economic performance. To those of us who regard the competitive policy primarily as a safeguard against the political consequences of concentrated power, it is insufficient for an additional reason. The big government and the big unions which Professor Galbraith regards as counterweights to big business may appear to be no more desirable than the big business they are expected to curb. We may doubt that a struggle among barons is the equivalent of democracy.

Fourth, Mr. Kaplan's argument that the power of the big is

---

[1] Some big companies emphasize publicly the large numbers of small concerns from which they buy and to which they sell. Their purpose is to show that large and small companies are inter-dependent. The more fully this is true, however, the less effective countervailing power can be in limiting the strength of the big.

inherently unstable rests upon an insecure basis. His principal evidence is that there have been many changes in the relative size of the larger companies, which he attributes primarily to competition in providing new products and developing new markets. That there is some competition of this kind among the big and that it may result in changes in relative industrial strength is obvious. But the variations in the relative size of large industrial companies are due to many other influences as well, among them mergers, anti-trust dissolutions, growth of different industries at different rates, and changes in the importance of different segments of the economy under the impact of war and depression. Nobody knows what importance competition among the big may have had in contributing to the changes. Moreover, in its most favorable light Mr. Kaplan's evidence indicates no more than that the big companies have jockeyed for position among themselves with varying results. He offers nothing to show that as a group they have declined significantly in absolute or relative size, or that, apart from the rise of new industries and without mergers, there have been significant cases in which genuinely small concerns became genuinely large ones; or that there have been any cases in which a genuinely large company was reduced to a genuinely small one. Nothing in his evidence discredits the view that difference in power creates between big companies and little companies a gap that is difficult to cross.[1]

Fifth, Mr. Kaplan's second point, that internal pressures to compete are generated within large companies, is more solid. Within the great corporation there are conflicting interests that often prevent it from acting as a monolith of power. Some of these interests are best served by vigorous expansion and hence possibly by competition. They may sometimes overcome the restrictive

---

[1] For a more detailed criticism of Kaplan's position, see a review of his book by Corwin D. Edwards in *University of Pennsylvania Law Review*, May 1955, pp. 991-998.

purposes of other intracorporate groups, and sometimes, though nominally defeated, thwart and sabotage these purposes. The internal disunity of a powerful concern may be a competitive force. Monopolistic purposes may fail by the slip between cup and lip. But is it also possible that the internal interests that favor restriction may win. Mr. Kaplan's argument shows, not the competitiveness of big business, but the complexity of the forces that are in conflict.

In summary, the case for big business has substantial elements of strength, particularly as to competitive innovation, competition in quality, inter-industry competition, and long-run price policy. There are important instances of competition in all these respects. The best performance by large enterprises is admirable. But policies that are restrictive and monopolistic are found alongside those that are competitive. The behavior of large enterprises is too diverse to justify blanket approval or disapproval.

Part of this diversity appears to be due to the fact that there are several types of big business, different in the sources of their power and in their characteristic behavior. The automobile companies have concentrated on the techniques of mass production, with attention to such matters as precisely articulated processes, continuous flow of materials from one process to the next, substitution of mechanical energy for human energy, and simplification of tasks. The big chemical companies have given primary attention to research, to the development of new processes and products evolved through research, and to the exploitation of patents. The large cigarette companies have emphasized advertising and related forms of salesmanship. The large dairy companies have become big primarily by merger and have done much to consolidate their power by political manipulation of sanitary laws, union contracts, and agreements with farm organizations. A monopoly of aluminum was supported for decades by control of the most accessible water-power sites and bauxite deposits.

Companies so different in the sources of their strength could not be expected to have uniform policies toward patent licensing, product development, price adjustment, quality control, or cost reduction. Diversity of interest has prevented them from developing a common point of view. This fact may have strengthened the tendencies toward competition with each other which were inherent in their desire to grow and in the dynamic influences of the economy. On the other hand, it may have facilitated agreements to allocate fields of activity and thus avoid competition. From time to time particular companies have attained sheltered positions of power and have exploited these positions in their several ways. In dealings with one another, the big companies have sometimes competed, sometimes acted jointly, and sometimes allocated their fields of activity so that each obtained full control of its own domain.

In spite of the diversity that is apparent in the patterns of big business, conclusions useful for our purpose can be drawn. We cannot label all big business competitive or anti-competitive. But from Chapter II we can conclude that anti-competitive and abusive excercises of power are common among big enterprises. Similarly, from this chapter we can conclude that, although the competitiveness of large companies has been exaggerated and the virtues of their economic performance have been overstated, there are important instances in which big companies compete vigorously in ways useful to the public. In the light of Chapter II our policy toward big business cannot wisely be based upon a sweeping approval of the big. In the light of this chapter it cannot wisely be based upon a sweeping condemnation. We must find something more discriminating than a comprehensive yes or no.

CHAPTER IV

THE DIRECTION OF PUBLIC POLICY

This chapter will discuss the public policy that is appropriate to the problem of big business. Like the analysis contained in the previous chapters, upon which it is based, it will presuppose the soundness of the American approach to problems of power. It will assume the desirability of systems of checks and balances to prevent undue concentrations of power and the desirability of competition as the form of economic organization that provides appropriate checks and balances. From this point of view, public policy toward business should be designed to maintain competition, not to replace it by public regulation or by a non-competitive system of collective bargaining among business men or by a benevolent but non-competitive business oligarchy. So far as there may be conflict between competition and bigness, bigness rather than competition should give way.

This general line of policy does not require, however, that every activity now governed by competition must continue to be so governed. There may be instances in which good economic performance is inconsistent with competition; and therefore, in the future as in the past, there may be reason to set up certain regulated private monopolies or state undertakings. But such extensions of the public utility principle should continue to be exceptions to the general rule. They should not become so numerous that competition ceases to be the norm in economic life. Nothing has appeared in the analysis of big business to justify the belief that the performance of the economic system would be improved if competition were set aside generally; and even if this were the case, it is questionable whether we would choose to purchase a better economy at the cost of our liberties.

The Need for Selective Appraisal

If these preconceptions are valid, the central question about big business is whether it is never, always, or sometimes inconsistent with competition.

The appropriate conclusion on this point depends partly upon the degree of bigness that is to be considered. There is an obvious possibility that large companies might become so big and so few as to make competition impossible. Advocates of the competitive policy who attack big business as inherently anti-competitive do not think that this has already happened; if they thought so, their own attacks would seem to them to be too late. But they think there is imminent danger in concentration so great that 11 percent of our manufacturing is done by five companies and nearly 27 percent by fifty companies. This point is hotly controversial. Clearly, however, danger lies along the road of increasing concentration. If the percentages of business done by a few big companies should progressively increase, the danger that is now controversial would become self-evident, and the economy would eventually reach a Zaibatsu-like concentration under which competition would be impossible. If concentration were increasing at the catastrophic rate observed by Berle and Means in 1932, the danger would be imminent. Immediate measures would be necessary to halt or reverse the trend if competition were not to be destroyed.

For the moment, however, we can base our policy upon the fact that concentration is increasing at the slower rate recorded by the Federal Trade Commission for the period 1935-1950.[1] Were

---

[1] Since the Commission's data require less statistical inference than those from which certain private scholars have concluded that concentration is not increasing at all, they are accepted here as the most reliable now available. Even if this were not so, it would be foolish to base the precautions of a public policy upon the most optimistic of conflicting estimates.

this rate of increase to continue, by the year 2000 the largest two hundred manufacturing companies would produce about 50 percent of our total manufacturing output, as compared with about 40 percent in 1950. Though such a trend is in the direction of increased danger, the rate of change is slow enough to enable us to formulate our public policy more carefully than would be possible if we were confronted by immediate catastrophe.

For the time being, then, our policy can be based, not upon the trend of concentration statistics, but upon an estimate of the significance of present levels of concentration, derived not only from the statistics but from the behavior of large enterprises.

On the basis of their conduct and policies, big companies cannot be regarded as uniformly competitive or non-competitive. The abuses of power summarized in Chapter II demonstrate that the big often reduce or destroy competition. The best examples of competitive performance by large enterprises, summarized in Chapter III, show that some substantial degree of bigness has often been not only harmless to competition but useful to the economy. Neither sweeping approval nor sweeping condemnation can survive an examination of the facts. At present levels of concentration, the appraisal of big business must be selective.

The standards for a selective appraisal are easy to state, though hard to apply. Big companies should not be too few and too big. They should not have the power to exclude promising new concerns. They should not be able to destroy the independence of small companies. They should remain independent of each other and in competition with each other. Bigness that creates danger should be prevented when it contributes nothing to efficiency of operation and also when its only contribution to the efficiency of the large enterprise consists in shifting risks and costs from that enterprise to weaker concerns. Big companies should, however, be big enough to operate large technological processes, to adopt economical methods of shipment, to undertake substantial programs of research and development, to integrate vertically where efficiency is increased thereby, and, in general, to perform such useful functions as require large organizations. Where the attainment of this degree of bigness endangers competition, danger that is not imminent should be accepted, though with vigilance; but clear and present danger or actual damage to competition should not be passively accepted. Instead, where such danger or damage is encountered, an effort should be made to preserve efficiency without sacrificing other interests of the public. To this end, competition should be replaced not by unregulated private power but by public regulation.

But any curtailment of competition for the sake of efficiency or for any other virtue which big business is supposed to possess should be a matter of high policy, to be legislatively determined. As will appear later, the standard of competition is suited to law enforcement, while the standard of economic performance is not. Moreover, where competition is no longer to protect the public interest, alternative safeguards must be devised; unchecked private power cannot be accepted as an alternative.

If it were possible to define accurately the degrees and kinds of bigness that are functionally useful and the degrees and kinds of bigness that convey objectionable power, and if these two categories did not overlap, the simplest way to cope with the problem of big business would be to prohibit the latter. A legal ceiling for bigness would avoid the risk that by a concession here and a concession there we might destroy competition piecemeal without awareness of what we were doing. But the apparent simplicity of such a solution is illusory. In some cases bigness that is dangerous and bigness that is useful probably overlap. Moreover, neither type of bigness can be defined uniformly for the whole economy. One level of bigness is appropriate to the petroleum industry, a different level to the soap industry, and a still different one to the milk industry. The degree of bigness which is appropriate to the technology of a given industry changes from time to time as productive methods change. It may be affected by the development of assembly lines, by the substitution of electric energy for belt drives, by automation, and by a host of other influences. A limit upon size that would be appropriate to the automobile industry would be meaninglessly large for women's garments. A limit appropriate to the manufacture of biscuits and crackers would be hopelessly small for automobile manufacture. A limit suitable to the aluminum industry in 1930 might be unsuitable in 1955.

Such difficulties could be countered only by empowering an agency of government to fix different limits for bigness in different industries and to revise the limits in any industry when circumstances changed. In practice, of course, the power to set ceilings by industry would also be the power to classify corporations in particular industries, to control the relative growth of the largest companies in the economy, and to change the rate of growth of large companies, both individually and collectively. Discretion so broad in a matter so important would be, in itself, repugnant to the principle that we should avoid concentration of governmental power. Indeed, an economy in which a government agency exercised such authority might readily be described, not as competitive, but as comprehensively regulated.

Greater flexibility could be introduced into such a program by prescribing, not an absolute limit upon growth, but a point beyond which further growth must be justified. In this version, the idea was incorporated in 1951 in a program proposed by the Committee on Monopolies of the Twentieth Century Fund.[1] With one member dissenting, the Committee suggested:

---

[1] George Stocking & Myron Watkins, *Monopoly and Free Enterprise,* (New York, Twentieth Century Fund, 1951). This volume contains a report by the Twentieth Century Fund's Committee on Cartels and Monopoly, which at pp. 563-564, includes the recommendation. A similar

"If this situation is to be clarified, the law should be brought face to face with the problem of size. Recognition should be given to the principle that great size, involving substantial concentration, will be permitted if it can be justified in terms of performance in the public interest, prohibited if it cannot. This principle might be written into the law itself; it might be established through the process of interpretation . . . As a possible means of formulating the establishment of this principle, we propose for consideration the desirability of amending the Sherman Act to create a rebuttable presumption against the retention by any enterprise of a position that enables it to control more than a fixed percentage of the market for any product or related group of products. If an enterprise could then demonstrate, in anti-trust proceedings, that a higher degree of concentration would serve the public interest, it might be permitted to retain the necessary area of market control. Otherwise, it might be divided into separate units of more moderate size."

Even if the proposal were thus modified, however, it would give to some government agency the power to license bigness by determining the various levels beyond which different enterprises must justify their growth and by deciding for each concern whether the justification it had submitted was adequate. Measures so drastic might be appropriate to check galloping concentration, such as appeared to be upon us at the beginning of the 1930's. With time to discover whether less dangerous remedies will be sufficient, we can and should defer consideration of discretionary governmental action to set varying limits upon business size.

When the dangers that spring from bigness are closely examined, it becomes evident that no general rule can be sufficient to

---

suggestion was made by me in 1949 (Corwin D. Edwards, *Maintaining Competition,* New York, McGraw-Hill Book Co., 1949, pp. 131-132). It was based upon belief that concentration was growing more rapidly than now appears to be the case.

provide appropriate safeguards and remedies. The problem is often one of finding a delicate balance among conflicting considerations. The corrective measures to be applied are different, and sometimes opposite, in different cases. Three examples may illustrate this diversity.

1. Competition is endangered when big companies engaged in different industries agree that each will stay in its own field, avoiding direct competition with the others. Because of the weakness of small enterprises as checks upon large ones, competition among the big is important; and to offset the oligopolistic tendencies of many industries, potential competition between industries is important. From this statement of the problem it follows that diversification should be regarded as a means to invigorate competition and that tendencies toward diversification by large enterprises should be encouraged.

However, diversification appears in a different perspective when the relations of big companies to small ones are considered. A diversified enterprise can hold a specialized smaller concern at its mercy, and because small companies know this they often surrender their business independence even though no effort to discipline or destroy them has been made by the large diversified company. Thus diversification tends to impair competition between the large and the small. Moreover, diversification multiplies the opportunities to grow. Thus it increases the total size and total power of the biggest companies, the disparity in size between large and small companies, and the danger that Zaibatsu-like effects may ensue. These considerations suggest that efforts should be made to limit each big company to a functionally coherent group of activities. The principle of coherence was used as a guide in the 1930's in legislative and administrative action to dissolve public utility holding company systems.

If public policy is to cope with both types of danger to competition, it can have no general rule about diversification. We may

III

discourage diversification in a setting in which small business enterprises have retained competitive vigor but are in danger of losing it. We may foster diversification where it promises to re-introduce competition into industries that have developed an excessively concentrated control. We may discourage a broad program of diversification designed to add substantially to the power of one of our largest companies, yet encourage that same company or others less powerful to undertake relatively narrow programs of entry into monopolized industries. Once a specific problem has been explored, the bearing of diversification upon it is likely to be clear, even though neither approval nor disapproval can be given to diversification in general.

2. Vertical integration, too, has conflicting effects upon competition. Companies that differ substantially in the number of successive manufacturing processes which they undertake are likely to develop diversity of interest that prevents them from agreeing not to compete. Where vertical integration exists in varying degrees, collusive restraint of trade is unlikely to be a major problem. Moreover, competition between methods of doing business is valuable: For a vertically integrated company to compete with a non-integrated one is a good way to find out whether successive processes should or should not be under the same managerial control. In these ways, vertical integration may strengthen competition.

But vertical integration may also strengthen monopoly. As was noted in Chapter II, companies big enough to make for themselves the components of their end products are likely to obtain discriminatory advantages in their buying. There are various possibilities of abuse of power where a big company is both supplier and competitor, or both customer and competitor, of a small concern. The non-integrated victim may be squeezed or cut off in time of shortage.

To reconcile these different possibilities of vertical integration in a general rule would be hard; but in a particular setting, the relative importance of the conflicting effects of vertical integration can be appraised, so that the appropriate line of public policy may be determined.

3. The desire to grow also has dual effects. It usually checks some of the worst monopolistic abuses. A company that thinks it cannot grow has an incentive to set high prices, to avoid producing more than it is sure it can sell, and to conserve its capital by avoiding innovations. Conversely, the hope to sell more often provides an incentive for healthy competition. A fight for more business tends to keep prices down and to encourage improvements in the quality of what is sold. Hence if we wish to foster competition we should preserve the opportunities and incentives for business growth.

But when a large enterprise grows faster than the economy, concentration is increased, and the dangers to competition that are inherent in excessive concentration are brought nearer. If the biggest companies grew less rapidly than the economy as a whole, the dangers from concentration would, in time, solve themselves. To reduce the opportunities for growth by the big may thus be regarded as a precaution on behalf of the competitive policy.

If it were necessary to apply a single rule, advocates of limiting bigness, even if big concerns were thereby encouraged to behave like monopolies, probably would disagree irreconcilably with advocates of stimulating growth even if it intensifies concentration. In specific situations, however, some types of growth by some companies may be forbidden without destroying useful incentive, and some kinds of opportunity to grow may be fostered without unduly increasing the dangers to competition.

Tests of Competition versus Performance Tests

For lack of a ceiling upon size or a uniform way to identify objectionable types and degrees of bigness, we must cope with the problems of big business case by case. Our method should be that of the anti-trust laws, which state broad objectives, but apply no general rules except rules of procedure. With a broad purpose to prevent accumulation and use of power that unnecessarily jeopardizes competition, we should investigate particular aggregates of power that appear to be dangerous, and when the danger is confirmed we should reduce the power or curb its exercise as the facts of the particular situation may suggest. Our attack should be selective, not comprehensive. The scope of the challenge to bigness should depend upon the frequency with which bigness, when specifically scrutinized, deserves challenge.

In recent years there has been clamor for an alternative principle, one which would invoke a test of economic performance in determining whether or not a company had violated the anti-trust laws.[1] As ordinarily advocated, such a test would be designed, not to create new offenses, but to permit the escape of some who might be convicted of reducing competition. Under the performance test, the government would be expected to prove that competition has been damaged, and in the absence of such proof there would be no violation of law. But whereas under the competitive principle proof of injury to competition is sufficient, under the performance principle the government would be expected to

---

[1] Some advocates of this idea have spoken of it incorrectly as the "rule of reason" approach, apparently on the assumption that the rule of reason means that what is reasonable is not illegal. The rule of reason has been a means of dividing offenses under the anti-trust laws into two groups, of which one includes practices that necessarily and substantially reduce competition and therefore are obviously unlawful, while the other includes practices whose effect upon competition is uncertain and must be discovered by a rational examination of the circumstances. The second group is said to be subject to the rule of reason approach. The difference between it and the first group lies in the nature of the evidence required, not in the test of legality, which, for both, is the substantial lessening of competition.

prove further that in the circumstances of the particular case the reduction of competition had resulted (or would result) in worse economic performance than before. The defendant would be acquitted if the government failed to establish this additional point. Thus the performance test is necessarily based upon the view that the purposes of the competitive policy are economic only and that the politicial considerations underlying the law have no relevance. It also presupposes that bad economic results cannot be reasonably inferred from impairment of competition, but must be separately shown. It would be a revolutionary departure from our present policy.

The effect of the performance test would be to substitute broad and complex issues for relatively simple ones.

Where price-fixing conspiracy is charged, for example, the decision now turns upon a question of fact—whether or not the defendants actually agreed upon prices. If the agreement is proved, the violation is established. Under the performance test, proof that prices had been fixed would be necessary but not sufficient. The government would also have to prove that the price fixing had been economically bad. Presumably the decision of this second point would turn upon two questions, first, whether or not it was economically desirable that prices be fixed at all, and second, whether the prices that had actually been fixed were reasonable prices. In approaching either of these questions, inference and economic philosophy would take the central place now occupied by evidence. To ascertain the economic effect of the fixed price, one would necessarily speculate what the price would have been if the price fixer had not acted. To evaluate that effect one would have to make the types of decision that have plagued public utility commissions in rate cases—whether prices should be set to promote expansion or to provide a fair return; whether a fair return should be computed upon normal, average, or actual volume of business; what should be considered a fair rate of return; whether capital values should be computed at original cost, replacement cost, or prudent investment. Such matters are settled by argument, not by evidence. Guilt in a price fixing case would depend upon the answers given by the courts to such speculative and philosophical issues.

The Hartford-Empire Case[1] may be offered as a contrast between present methods of law enforcement and those appropriate to a performance test. The courts found that patents covering the manufacture of glass bottles had been pooled under a profit-sharing arrangement and had then been used to allocate fields of bottle manufacture. Manufacturers were given licenses for types of bottles they already made, but were not authorized to encroach further upon one another. Fields in which there was only one maker were exclusively licensed. Newcomers were excluded from licenses except where there was an admitted shortage of a particular type of bottle. Where two or more companies produced the same type of bottle, their interests were reconciled by quotas. This scheme was found to be in violation of the anti-trust laws because it set aside competition to an extent not authorized by patent law.

Under the performance test, evidence as to economic developments in the industry would have been relevant. The defense would have shown that from 1928 to 1938 the price of fruit jars declined 10 percent; the price of milk bottles 13.9 percent; the price of medicinal ware 25 percent; the price of glass food containers 34 percent. It would have shown an increase in the industry's productive capacity from 56 million gross in 1930, of which 57 percent was used, to 80 million gross in 1940, of which 68 percent was used. It would have shown that small enterprises had increased their percentage of industry shipments from 20 to 32; that average hourly wages had risen between 1929 and 1935 from

---

[1] *U.S. v. Hartford Empire Co.,* 323 U.S. 386.

50 cents to 71 cents, and that average working hours per week had fallen from 49.7 to less than 39.[1] On the basis of such figures the defense would undoubtedly have argued that no bad economic performance could be shown.

The prosecutor's answer to the claim probably would have been that the decline in prices was attributable to the great depression that began in 1929; the expansion of capacity and the greater sales by small producers were results of the repeal of the prohibition amendment in 1933; and the improvements in wages and hours were the results of New Deal labor legislation and of the strengthening of unions that accompanied it. But for the allocation plan, the prosecution probably would have argued, the industry's showing would have been better. Of course the defense would have rejected these arguments.

The guilt of the defendants would then have depended upon the court's conclusion as to the relative effects of the depression, repeal of prohibition, labor legislation, and the allocation of patent licenses in furthering or retarding the industry's economic performance.

If the courts were required in each case to compare the conduct of defendants with hypothetical alternatives and then to evaluate the desirability of the consequences thus attributed to the defendants, there would be no end to the speculative possibilities and consequently no limit to the burden of proof that a conscientious court would have to impose upon the prosecutor. A trial is not the proper means to settle a clash of predictions or a broad conflict of economic opinions. The probable effect, if the performance test were taken seriously, would be the breakdown of the anti-trust laws.

---

[1] Walter Adams, and others, *The Structure of American Industry,* (New York, Macmillan Co., 1950). Chapter 11, The Glass Container Industry, pp. 305-341.

But there is a second possibility. Desiring to try anti-trust cases in a finite time and to make the law work if possible, the courts might arbitrarily simplify the complicated issues set before them. They might evolve a set of legal presumptions as to what would have happened if the defendants had not interfered and as to what economic results are desirable in given circumstances. Whether such legal short cuts to an economic philosophy would satisfy economists is problematical. But the breakdown of the anti-trust laws might be thus averted.

In that case, there would be time for a second effect to appear. This would be the complete abandonment of the principle of competition. If proof of bad economic performance is the essential element in a prosecution, prosecutors will soon object to the additional burden of proving lack of competition. If companies are to be prosecuted for bad economic performance, there is little logic in attacking only the bad economic performance that ensues when competition is lessened. The simple and appropriate expression of the performance test is to apply the law to any bad economic result that is avoidable, no matter how it originated. Thus we may expect that if the performance test were to be used successfully, it would soon evolve into a requirement that business avoid bad economic results or be appropriately disciplined. Such a requirement would be a legal basis for unlimited government intervention in business. It would be more suited to a comprehensive system of public control than to an economy of free private competitive enterprise.

The guiding principle of the anti-trust laws, therefore, should continue to be the preservation of competition. Where this principle is to be limited, the action should be taken by the Congress, which can provide alternative safeguards, not by the courts in the day-to-day administration of the law. Even the Congress should be careful that exceptions do not become numerous enough to deprive the economy of its predominantly competitive tone.

The Need for More Information

The first requisite of a case-by-case approach to the problem of bigness, based on the competitive principle and on the anti-trust laws, is information. When the investigation of a large enterprise has begun the courts and commissions have adequate power to get the relevant facts. But we lack the information we need in deciding when to investigate and in considering whether our piecemeal remedies are successful. We should regularly obtain enough information about big business to detect situations that might be dangerous and to take action about them before great harm is done. Such information is not now available.

Several kinds of information are needed. Some government agency should report fully and regularly the facts about business concentration. The trend of concentration seems to have changed between the period studied by Berle and Means and the period covered by the Federal Trade Commission report upon which these suggestions as to policy rely. The trend may change again, and if so public policy should adapt itself to the new facts without undue delay.

Regular reports of the level of concentration should be regarded as necessary tools of public policy in the same sense that regular reports of wholesale prices and employment are now so regarded. Although the Federal Trade Commission has indicated publicly that it contemplates furnishing concentration figures at frequent intervals, the aspiration has not yet been bolstered by a publication schedule, assigned personnel, and a regular appropriation. Indeed, a report currently in progress at the Commission appears to have been deferred for other work. Estimates of the trend of concentration still depend upon uncoordinated studies made at various dates by various agencies, public and private, and differing in purpose, scope, statistical procedures, and reliability.

The quality of the figures on concentration should be greatly improved. Particularly, the figures should be segregated and combined to conform more closely to the boundaries of competitive markets; enough information about ownership should be provided to throw light upon the competition of substitutes; and means should be developed to measure the size of conglomerate and vertically integrated firms. The conceptual and statistical difficulties in such work are substantial; they cannot be solved by casual or intermittent effort. Responsibility for concentration figures produced by the government should be assigned; adequate funds and personnel should be made regularly available; and problems of concept and method should be worked out by conference with interested public and private agencies. Until this is done, those responsible for policy toward concentrated business power must operate in a twilight of knowledge.

Large enterprises should be required to give the public more information about their activities than they now supply. Basic facts about the sales, profits, assets and debts of a large company are matters of public concern, affecting not only many stockholders and employees, but also many persons dependant on dealings with the company, and even the government which must protect the policy of competition. Yet some large interstate corporations—for example, Ford Motor Company and Lever Brothers —publish no annual financial statements. In spite of the requirement that such data be furnished by companies that are listed on registered securities exchanges or offer their security issues to the public in interstate commerce, the companies with assets of $5 million or more which do not publish financial statements are almost as numerous as those which do. Moreover, almost without exception big companies that operate in several industries and control many subsidiaries publish only consolidated figures, so that the public cannot ascertain the sales or profits attributable to different parts of the business. The financial statement of a diversified big company cannot provide information equivalent to that in the financial statements of small specialized companies unless the large company's statement is departmentalized. Corporations large enough to be capable of creating problems under the policy of competition should be subject to a requirement that they publish specified financial and statistical information that can help determine whether such problems actually exist.

Such corporations should also be required to disclose who controls them. Corporate charters may be conceived as legal false faces, behind which, if enough masks are removed, there are real people. In many instances, those who actually control a corporation are known to be particular owners of stock or particular managers representing many owners. There are cases, however, in which the corporate mask is used to deceive both the government and those who deal with the corporation. A subsidiary enterprise poses as independent; two or more affiliated concerns pretend to be unrelated; transactions that are actually within the corporate family masquerade as arm-length dealings; foreigners pretend to be natives, or natives foreigners. Without knowing what companies are part of the same community of interest, nobody can correctly evaluate big business. Disclosures of ownership adequate to throw light upon control and upon interlocking interests should be required from each large corporation. These disclosures should include (a) the names of the largest stockholders in the corporation, with the amount of their holdings; and (b) the names of companies in which the corporation holds stock, with the amount of each holding.

Corporate ties may be established, of course, by other means than stock ownership—by interlocking directorates, common officerships, management contracts, exclusive dealing arrangements, comprehensive agreements to pool technology, and various other devices. No effort will be made here to state how far disclosure of such matters should be carried in order to provide an accurate picture of the impact of concentration, nor what precautions should be taken to assure the continued confidentiality of trade secrets. As to some of these matters there could be too much disclosure as well as too little. But if we are to cope with problems of concentration intelligently, enough must be disclosed about the big companies to indicate how far their influence reaches. To work out the details of such a requirement is properly the task of an administrative agency empowered to study concentration problems continuously.[1]

The Importance of Curbing Mergers

Granted adequate information, the second requisite for a discriminating approach to the problem of bigness is to erect a barrier against further increases in concentration. If we were to move toward levels of concentration that are clearly inconsistent with competition, we would find it necessary in the future either to abandon the policy of competition or to take the drastic steps necessary to reverse the concentrative trend. But these steps are hard to take. Dissolution, divorcement, and divestiture, however appropriate they may be, entail temporary disruption of business and economic loss, and the courts, aware of the responsibility they incur, are always reluctant to use such drastic remedies. Excessive concentration of power is much harder to destroy than to prevent. We should retain whatever leeway the existing levels of concentration have left us. Hence we should try to prevent the large corporations, as a group, from growing more rapidly than the economy grows. But we must do this in ways that leave each corporation free to attempt to grow; for, as has already been stated, the incentive to grow is one of the most vigorous incentives

---

[1] The foregoing suggestions are not intended to imply that business, or even large business, should operate "in a gold-fish bowl." The purpose is merely to suggest that corporations big enough that their bigness might adversely affect competition should disclose what must be known in order to determine how big they are, who controls them, and with what other corporations they are affiliated.

to compete. We must take the risk that concentration will increase dangerously through the internal expansion of large corporations. We must limit the average rate of growth of the big companies, not by attacking growth as such, but by selecting for attack those types of growth that are seldom functionally useful and often injurious to competition.

Growth by merger is an outstanding example of functionless and dangerous growth. When one competitor acquires another, there is little chance that the properties of the two, originally designed for separate operation, can be effectively coordinated as a single operating unit. But there is a probability that if either concern is large competition will be reduced by the acquisition. One of the big units becomes bigger; the number of competitors is reduced; and the merging corporation expands in a way that does not expand the industry. Though particular instances can doubtless be found in which such a merger is harmless, the typical result must be that efficiency is not well served and competition is ill served. Growth achieved by this means is not limited by a market struggle for public favor, as is the ordinary expansion of sales. Hence this kind of growth is peculiarly likely to outrun the growth of the economy.

Vertical and conglomerate mergers are less clearly objectionable than mergers of competitors, and the instances in which they actually do no harm are more numerous. But such mergers, too, are properly subject to suspicion. They, too, can readily enable a big company to outstrip the growth of the economy by means that do not reflect efficiency of operation, customer preferences, and competitive success. They can impair competition by depriving competitors of access to the most desirable sources of supply or the most effective marketing channels.

It was wise, therefore, to enact the Celler-Kefauver Anti-Merger Act of 1950.[1] Under this statute acquisitions of corporate

---

[1] 64 *Stat.* 1125.

assets or stock by another corporation may be enjoined where damage to competition is reasonably probable. Since the law turns upon the probability of a future effect, vigorous enforcement of it probably will prevent a few acquisitions that are innocent or even beneficial. But in addition to blocking many mergers that would be immediately harmful to competition, it will tend to limit the growth of the big companies, and thus to prevent increase in the concentration of economic power, in the way that is most consistent with the preservation of healthy corporate incentives. If it proves sufficient to keep the rate of growth of the big companies below the rate of growth of the economy, it will prevent us from having to make hard choices between undesirable forms of government intervention in corporate affairs and levels of concentration that endanger competition.

But if this statute is to have an important part in our public policy, it must be enforced more vigorously than it has been during its first four years. Detecting dangerous mergers and demonstrating their probable effects is not easy. It cannot be done by a few people. Yet the Congress has appropriated little for the task, and in mid-1955 the Federal Trade Commission, which carries the major responsibility for enforcing the anti-merger law, was able to assign to this work the equivalent of only eighteen full-time professional employees. Though we are in the midst of the third great merger movement of this century, only six proceedings under the statute had been initiated by the Commission and the Department of Justice prior to July 1, 1955. More effective enforcement at this point is essential if we are to avoid the harsher subsequent remedies of dissolution and if other forms of corporate growth are to remain unchallenged.

Encouragement of Voluntary Divestiture

A third requisite for a discriminating approach to the problem of bigness is encouragement for big companies to slough off portions of their activities. A big diversified concern is seldom wholly coordinated. Some of the properties it has acquired or built do not fit into the general structure. Some of the activities it carries on contribute little to the rest and would be more efficient if they were independently operated. In such instances it would often be efficient to organize part of the business as a separate corporation and to dispose of the large concern's ownership by distribution of the new company's stock to stockholders of the old company. Nobody can identify such possibilities as well as the managements of the companies in which they exist. If managements could be induced to undertake such appropriate divestitures,[1] their action might appreciably lessen the problems associated with bigness. Less alarm need be felt over a big company's growth in some directions if there is shrinkage in others, particularly if the two processes result in no great change in the company's total size.

Until recently the sloughing off of parts of a corporate structure was discouraged by tax laws that treated the accompanying distributions of stock as income to the stockholders. Consequently, nobody knows whether voluntary divestiture could go far enough to have a significant effect upon the concentration of power. Today such a distribution of stock is no longer thus penalized. This is movement in the right direction. But it is not sufficient. The government should make its approval of voluntary divestiture clear and emphatic. It should seek means to overcome the inertia and self-interest of corporate managements so far as these are obstacles. The top executives of large corporations have a human desire not to reduce their power by voluntarily reducing the size of their domain; and direct pecuniary incentives are likely to be needed to overcome this attitude. We should experiment with

---

[1] An example of voluntary action along these lines is the decision of United Aircraft Corporation to organize part of its business as a separate corporation, Chance-Vought Aircraft. The stock of the latter company was distributed to United Aircraft stockholders in 1954.

legislation that reduces tax burdens when parts of corporations are voluntarily divested. We should explore the question whether other types of incentive can be created—for example, whether requirements such as are suggested above, that large companies disclose the facts about their ownership and activities, can be varied with size so that reduction of a company's assets reduces its obligation to disclose. If cooperation can be obtained, it is foolish to rely wholly upon coercive techniques in limiting corporate power.

Prevention of Joint Action by The Big

One of the most important requisites of a discriminating policy toward big business is a determined effort to prevent big companies from acting concertedly to enhance and consolidate their control over their fields of operation. Agreements create an aggregate of power roughly measured by the total size of those who have agreed. When the big agree on matters that ought to be competitively determined, they destroy the chance that one big company will check another; they thus convert big business into a comprehensive monopolistic arrangement. Use of the anti-trust laws against restrictive conspiracies should be especially vigilant in the case of large corporations.

The most dangerous type of conspiracy among the big is the allocation agreement. In such a scheme, big companies reciprocally promise one another that each will confine itself to the markets reserved for it, so that none will compete with another. Whereas price agreements often break down and agreements on quotas of output are hard to reach, allocation agreements are easily achieved wherever the participants do not already have a serious overlap of interests. Such agreements tend to become stronger as time passes, and their importance to the participants facilitates the development of other types of anti-competitive agreement for markets that cannot readily be allocated.[1] The prevention of allocation arrangements among the big is the most important aspect of anti-trust policy.

But anti-competitive collaboration among the big does not always take the form of a contract. A working understanding may be expressed in corporate structure, for example through the organization of a jointly owned subsidiary to conduct the business that two or more large corporations have in common. Where the sole purpose of joint ownership is to avoid competition, such a subsidiary can be and should be dissolved without hesitancy. In some instances, however, the jointly owned company is a device to pool the resources and the technology of corporations which are not severally equipped for the task at hand. A petrochemical company, for example, may be organized jointly by a petroleum company and a chemical company and may thus combine the two types of experience needed in exploring a new field. There is no need to handicap development by forbidding such joint ventures. Nevertheless, this type of arrangement is likely to preclude competition between concerns that are potentially competitors and to result eventually in fewer business units in the new field than might otherwise appear there. Hence such joint control by big companies should be regarded as temporary. After a reasonable period of time the collaborating companies should be required to terminate their partnership by making the subsidiary independent or by transfer of ownership to a single parent company or by some other appropriate means. Though cooperation in appropriate

---

[1] In practice there are often markets from which two or more companies are unwilling to withdraw. These become exceptions specifically provided for. In the early stages of an allocation scheme, they are usually excluded from the agreement and left open for competition. In later stages arrangements are usually made to share them by joint ownership of distributing corporations, quotas of sale, or other similar devices. See *U.S. v. Imperial Chemical Industries, Ltd., et al.,* 105 F. Supp. 215.

cases should be permitted, collaboration among the big should not be allowed to become so strong and enduring as to substitute a community of interest for a competitive relationship.

For similar reasons, stock ownership by large corporations should be kept under suspicious surveillance. So long as stock control that injures competition is a sporadic phenomenon, it can be attacked through the anti-merger law, which covers acquisitions of stock as well as assets. But there are indications that we are on the verge of a new kind of stock-holding community of interest among large companies. Pension funds established by large corporations are growing rapidly into great pools of investment capital, and in general are being invested in the securities of other corporations. So long as the investments are small, no problem arises. If they become large enough, they may create among many large companies reciprocal interests in the prospertiy of other concerns. Such developments should be watched, and curbed so far as may be found necessary.

The law as to personal interlocks among large companies should also be tightened. At present, an individual may not be director of two or more large companies that are in competition. But the law does not cover interlocks among corporate officials other than directors, nor does it prevent competitors from having directors drawn from the same bank, advertising agency, or law firm. Moreover, it does not curb interlocking directorates among concerns that are potential rather than actual competitors, and it does not cover the representation of competitors upon the directorates of suppliers and customers under conditions in which such representation could be the equivalent of a market-sharing agreement.[1]

It is probably impossible to formulate a practicable rule that

---

[1] See Federal Trade Commission, *Report on Interlocking Directorates*. (Washington, Government Printing Office, 1951.)

will be tight enough to eliminate all opportunities for collaboration through the interlocking representation of what ought to be conflicting interests.[1] But much more can be done than our public policy now provides.

Various other types of less formal collaboration among the big should also be prevented. Companies are unlikely to be competitors in their present activities or potential competitors in future activities if they use the same trade mark. Deliberate sharing of trade marks should be prevented; and steps should be taken to eliminate joint use of marks by big companies in the instances in which such use was initially accidental. Similarly, means should be found to reconcile exchange of technology with competition among companies that are parties to the exchange. This problem, which involves most of the intracacies of the patent law and of its relation to the anti-trust laws,[1] is too complicated for adequate discussion here. It is clear, however, that the power inherent in large aggregates of patents controlled by a single company exceeds

---

[1] It is, of course, foolish to try to prevent personal contacts among persons who direct rival corporations. Such contacts can be established in any club house or lunch room. The rule as to interlocking directorates rests upon the principle that persons with official responsibility for corporate policy should not occupy positions in which they simultaneously represent interests that ought to be in conflict or in which the mere performance of the official duties of their various posts has the effect of establishing an agreement on policy that would be unlawful if more formally reached. The proposal here is that this principle be more comprehensively applied. It would be easy to change the law so that a director of one company could not be president of a competitor; it would be harder, but still possible, to provide that competitors might not have as directors different officials of the same bank and that competitors might not share the directorate of a supplier whose business could be thereby allocated among them. It probably would be impossible to prevent competitors from collaborating through directors who were brothers or cousins.

[1] See Corwin D. Edwards, *Maintaining Competition,* (New York, McGraw Hill Publishing Co., 1949) pp. 216-248.

that conveyed by any one patent and that the power achieved when two or more companies pool such aggregates is still larger. Monopolistic exercise of power based upon such aggregates of patents can now be curbed by the anti-trust laws, and patent control can be relaxed where such action is an appropriate corrective for law violation; but prevention of collaborative activities based upon exchange of patents, as distinguished from subsequent correction, is not now possible. Problems as to the right to withhold patents from use by would-be licensees and the restrictions that may be imposed upon a licensee should be considered, with suitable distinction between the single patent and the large aggregate of patents. A principal purpose should be to prevent big companies from including in cross licenses of their technology conditions that allocate fields or otherwise prevent competition among the participants in the cross-licensing plan.

Summary

In broad summary then, an appropriate public policy toward the danger from big business in a competitive system should rely primarily upon case-by-case procedure under the anti-trust laws. Large companies that possess and abuse power should be subject, as they now are, to two types of corrective action. Where the abuse is not inherent in the fact that excessive power has been concentrated, punitive and injunctive proceedings should be used to eliminate the abuse. Where the power is so great that it is inherently inconsistent with competition, and where the available correctives of corporate behavior have been tried and have failed, the drastic remedies of divestiture, divorcement, and dissolution should be used

But this existing policy should be strengthened and supplemented in various ways. Provision should be made to obtain and analyze more basic information showing who controls large companies, what size and power these companies have achieved, and how they are related to each other. This information is needed both to determine where investigation is needed and to ascertain whether the policy as a whole is proving reasonably successful.

In applying the anti-trust laws, particular attention should be given to the law against mergers that injure competition, in order to limit the growth of big companies and forestall disastrous increases in the concentration of economic power without destroying the healthy incentive to grow. For this same purpose, an effort should be made, by changes in the tax laws and perhaps by other means as well, to encourage large corporations to divest themselves voluntarily of those parts of their business that can readily stand alone.

Special efforts should be made to preserve competition among big companies. To this end, the anti-trust laws should be used vigorously against restrictive agreements among the big, particularly agreements to allocate fields of business. The laws should be strengthened to prevent structural arrangements among big companies that foster monopolistic collaboration. The use of joint subsidiaries should be confined to instances where the facilities and knowledge of the parent companies are inadequate unless pooled, and even under such conditions the collaboration should be temporary. Precautions should be taken against corporate communities of interest based upon interlocking investments. The law against interlocking directorates should be greatly tightened. Preventive measures should be applied to other forms of anti-competitive collaboration, such as joint use of trade marks and the use of commercial restrictions to facilitate technological exchanges among holders of large numbers of patents.

The guiding principle in such a policy toward big business should continue to be the maintenance of competition for political as well as economic reasons. The test of legality should not be the quality of business performance, but the existence of adequate competition. We should recognize, however, that a large enterprise is enabled to lessen or destroy competition by its own possession of economic power; and our concept of power should be broadened to fit the facts of big business. We should cease to pay exclusive attention to monopoly power, as distinguished from types of power, summarized in Chapter Two, that are traceable to bigness instead of monopoly. We should cease to smuggle other types of power into our thinking by calling them monopoly power. We should accept the fact that power may be derived from oligopolistic or monopolistic place in a signficant market, from disparity in size between competing corporations or between buyer and seller, from structural forms such as vertical integration or diversification, and from the aggregate bigness of a corporation's activities as a whole. None of these types of power is unvarying in its effect; each may be present in different degrees; and each may be reinforced by other types of power possessed by the same company and may be reduced or increased by the power of other companies. We can rely upon no simple formula for detecting power or for determining where it has become so great that it must be curbed. But where we can identify power that impairs competition, we should strike it down.

With such a public policy it may be that we can accept the constructive achievements of big business, yet curb the anti-competitive tendencies that are apparent in the concentration of economic power. Our chance to do so will be improved if we approach big business with neither adulation nor fear, but with the cool mixture of receptiveness and suspicion with which a business executive would himself approach a problem in which he saw both opportunities and dangers. It may be that the effort to reconcile big business and competition will fail, and that we may some day find it necessary to choose between bigness and the competitive policy. But that time is not yet; and with care to keep ourselves informed, we must leave the future's problems to be met by the future's vigilance.

APPENDIX

Violations of Anti-Monopoly Laws by Fifty
Largest Industrial Companies

Table I covers proceedings by the Department of Justice. For each case (or closely related group of cases based upon the same subject matter) column one of the tabulation gives the serial number under which the case appears in the semi-official summary of cases issued by Commerce Clearing House[1] and in the mimeographed supplements to that summary issued by the Department of Justice. Column two names such of the defendants as were among the largest fifty industrial companies in 1948 (including in a few instances, certain predecessors or subsidiaries of such large companies). Where the company named is a predecessor or subsidiary, the fact is noted. For cases that have been finally adjudicated,[2] column three contains the year of the final judgment; for cases still pending, it indicates that fact. For pending cases, it also states whether the proceedings are civil or criminal. For cases that have been completed, column four indicates by what process the

---

[1] The Federal Anti-trust Laws with Summary of Cases, *op. cit.*

[2] Where cases were appealed, final adjudication is conceived as completion of appellate review of the case. Where there were separate settlements as to individual defendants, the date of settlement for defendants mentioned in the table has been selected if ascertained. Under civil decrees the court often retains jurisdiction and subsequently modifies the decree; in such instances, the original decree has been regarded as closing the case. Interim decrees intended to apply for a brief period have not been regarded, however, as terminating the cases to which they apply.

decision against the defendant was reached. In some instances, the defendant was convicted after trial (including whatever appeal may have been made from lower court decisions). In some instances the defendant pleaded nolo contendere (in a criminal proceeding) or consented to the entry of a decree (in a civil proceeding), but did not formally admit guilt. Column five summarizes the offense which was involved in the case. The summaries are too brief to be complete, and in some instances they have been made technically inaccurate in order to convey the essence of the charge in a few words. Moreover, the reader should bear in mind that where there was a plea of nolo contendere or a consent decree, the statement of the offense necessarily rests upon a formal accusation, not a judicial finding or a jury's verdict. Though one may fairly presume that the defendant would have contested the case if he could have expected to win, one cannot be certain that no part of the government's charge could have been refuted. For cases that have been completed, column six states the nature of the remedy or penalty invoked. Where a fine was levied, the case was criminal; where an injuction was issued, or dissolution or divestiture was ordered, the case was civil, and where both were applied, there were companion civil and criminal cases. Column seven contains such additional remarks as may throw light upon the significance of the proceeding, especially reference to unusual features of injunctions and mention of the lower court decision in cases that are pending on appeal.

TABLE I: DEPARTMENT OF JUSTICE CASES (INCLUDING CASES PENDING)
PETROLEUM

I Serial Number of Case	II Names of Defendant Companies	III Date of Final Disposition	IV Method of Decision	V Offense Charged	VI Penalty or Remedy Applied	VII Remarks
41	Standard Oil Co. of New Jersey, predecessor of present Standard Oil Co. (N.J.)	1911	Conviction after trial.	Monopolistic combination maintained by purchase of competitors, secret rebates on transportation, local price cutting to destroy competitors, operating bogus independents, etc.	Dissolution.	
369	Standard Oil of California. Texas Co.	1930	Consent decree	Conspiracy to fix gasoline prices on Pacific Coast.	Injunction.	Decree modified 1933, to permit operation under NRA code.
415 419	Standard Oil (Ind.) Socony-Vacuum Oil. Sinclair Oil. Phillips Petroleum	1940-1941	Plea of nolo contendere (Standard) Conviction after trial (Others)	Conspiracy to raise price of gasoline in Mid-Continent and East Texas fields.	Fines.	
420	Standard Oil (Ind.) Socony-Vacuum Oil. Texas Co. Sinclair Oil. Phillips Petroleum.	1941	Pleas of nolo contendere.	Conspiracy to fix jobbers' margins on gasoline in ten mid-western states.	Fines.	

I Serial Number of Case	II Names of Defendant Companies	III Date of Final Disposition	IV Method of Decision	V Offense Charged	VI Penalty or Remedy	VII Remarks
			PETROLEUM (CONTINUED)			
465	Standard Oil of California. Texas Co. Shell Oil.	1940	Pleas of nolo contendere.	Conspiracy to fix gasoline prices on Pacific Coast by buying gasoline produced by independents.	Fine.	
532	Shell Oil.	1941	Plea of nolo contendere.	Conspiracy to select bidders and control bids in emulsified asphalt for state projects in Georgia.	Fine.	
695, 696	Standard Oil (N.J.)	1942	Plea of nolo contendere. Consent decree.	Agreement with I. G. Farben industrie not to compete and to allocate fields. Use of combined patents to prevent others from making improved products.	Fine. Injunction.	Decree includes royalty-free licensing of patents on production of synthetic gasoline and rubber; compulsory licensing of catalytic refining patents at reasonable royalty.
883	Standard Oil of California.	1949	Conviction after trial.	Exclusive dealing contracts with service stations, covering petroleum products and automobile accessories.	Injunction.	

No.	Defendants	Year	Result	Charge	Penalty	Disposition
890, 891 (See also Motor vehicles and Rubber)	Standard Oil of California. Phillips Petroleum. General Motors. Firestone Tire & Rubber.	1955 (civil) 1951 (Cr.)	Conviction after trial (Standard). Dismissal (others). Conviction after trial (all).	Conspiracy to monopolize sale of gasoline, tires, motor buses, etc, to nation-wide combine of urban bus lines.	Injunction and Fines.	Standard enjoined from enforcing 3 contracts. Consent degree against bus lines. Others dismissed in civil action.
1024	Standard Oil of California. Texas Co. Shell Oil.	Civil Case Pending.	?	Conspiracy to monopolize crude petroleum and refined petroleum products in Pacific States Area: acquisition of independants, production quotas, pipe-line discrimination, price fixing.	Injunction and Fines.	?
1163	Standard Oil (N.J.) Standard Oil of California. Socony-Vacuum Oil. Gulf Oil. Texas Co.	Civil Case Pending.	?	World-wide cartel to limit production of crude oil and allocate markets and fix prices for refined petroleum products.		?

ELECTRICAL PRODUCTS

No.	Defendants	Year	Result	Charge	Penalty	Disposition
82	General Electric.	1911	Conviction after trial.	Control of sale of incandescent lamps by use of bogus independent companies and tying contracts to fix prices and eliminate competition.	Injunction.	Bogus independent companies dissolved by decree.

Electrical Products (Continued)

I Serial Number of Case	II Names of Defendant Companies	III Date of Final Disposition	IV Method of Decision	V Offense Charged	VI Penalty or Remedy Applied	VII Remarks
371	General Electric. Westinghouse Electric.	1932	Consent decree.	Conspiracy to monopolize radio communication by joint ownership and cross licensing of patents.	Injunction.	Decree includes requirement that General Electric and Westinghouse dispose of interest in RCA, and forbids exclusive licensing of relevant patents.
551	General Electric.	1941	Plea of nolo contendere.	Conspiracy by two American companies to pay two Dutch companies not to compete in the United States upon glass light bulbs.	Fine.	
575	Westinghouse Electric. General Electric.	1942	Consent decree. (Westinghouse)	Conspiracy to monopolize incandescent lamps, tubing, bulbs, and other electrical equipment; involved pooling patents, limiting production, allocating territory, price fixing, and eliminating competition.	Injunction.	Decrees provide dedication of lamp patents to public and compulsory license of certain future patents at reasonable royalty.
		1953	Conviction after trial. (General Electric)			

650	General Electric.	1948	Conviction after trial.	Conspiracy to monopolize hard metal alloys by pooling patents, eliminating imports and exports, excluding competitors, limiting production, alloting marketing territories, and fixing prices.	Fine.	
747	General Electric. Westinghouse Electric.	1954	Consent decree.	Conspiracy to monopolize fluorescent lamp trade, involving price fixing, eliminating imports by cartel agreement, stifling production by independents, and agreement with utility companies not to promote fluorescent lamps.	Injunction.	Decree provides for royalty-free compulsory licensing of patents, and licensing of certain future patents at reasonable royalty.
809	General Electric. Westinghouse Electric.	1948	Conviction after trial.	Conspiracy with licensees to fix prices on drop-out fuse cutouts.	Injunction.	
814	General Electric.	1953	Consent decree.	Conspiracy to divide world market on all types of electric equipment except lamps and radios, involving exclusive rights to U.S. market.	Injunction.	Decree includes compulsory licensing at reasonable royalty.

ELECTRICAL PRODUCTS (CONTINUED)

I Serial Number of Case	II Names of Defendant Companies	III Date of Final Disposition	IV Method of Decision	V Offense Charged	VI Penalty or Remedy Applied	VII Remarks
818	Westinghouse Electric.	1953	Consent decree.	Conspiracy with German interests to allocate trade territories on electrical equipment and exchange exclusive rights to technology.	Injunction.	Decree includes dedication of relevant patents to public.
834	General Electric.	1947	Consent decree.	Participation of export trade association in cartel arrangement to fix prices, allocate orders and eliminate competition.	Injunction.	
886	General Electric.	1948	Consent decree.	Conspiracy to fix prices of high tension cable through operation of patent pool. Suppression of a superior cable.	Injunction.	Decree includes compulsory licensing at nondiscriminatory royalties, including certain future patents.
915, 916	General Electric.	1949	Plea of nolo contendere and consent decree.	Conspiracy to fix prices on electric switches and equipment sold to public utility companies on West Coast.	Fine and injunction.	

	Company	Year	Disposition	Charge	Outcome
959, 960	General Electric.	1952	Plea of nolo contendere and consent decree.	Conspiracy to fix prices on street lighting equipment.	Fine and injunction.
971	Western Electric.	Civil Case Pending.	?	Monopoly of production of telephone equipment, based on requirement by parent company, American Telephone & Telegraph Co, that all telephone operating companies controlled by it must obtain equipment from Western Electric.	?

CHEMICALS

	Company	Year	Disposition	Charge	Outcome
51	E. I. duPont de Nemours, predecessor of present company.	1913	Conviction after trial.	Monopolistic combination attained by buying control of and dissolving competitors.	Dissolution.
613	E. I. duPont de Nemours. Allied Chemical & Dye.	1941	Consent decree.	Conspiracy to monopolize U.S. foreign trade in fertilizer nitrogen. Agreement on prices, quantities, and destinations of imports and exports.	Injunction.

CHEMICALS (CONTINUED)

I Serial Number of Case	II Names of Defendant Companies	III Date of Final Disposition	IV Method of Decision	V Offense Charged	VI Penalty or Remedy Applied	VII Remarks
706	E. I. duPont de Nemours. Allied Chemical & Dye.	1946	Pleas of nolo contendere.	Conspiracy to fix prices for dyestuffs, limit amounts sold by American manufacturers in foreign markets, and prevent small chemical manufacturers from participating in manufacture.	Fines.	
712	E.I. duPont de Nemours.	1943	Plea of nolo contendere.	Conspiracy to fix prices of commercial explosives.	Fine.	
717	E. I. duPont de Nemours.	1945	Plea of nolo contendere.	Conspiracy to fix prices of sulfuric acid, limit the quantity, control channels of distribution, induce small companies to discontinue production.	Fine.	
718	E.I. duPont de Nemours.	1945	Plea of nolo contendere.	Conspiracy to fix prices of chromic acid, limit production, allocate customers, and control channels of distribution.	Fine.	

No.	Company	Year	Plea/Outcome	Charge	Penalty	Decree
720	E.I. duPont de Nemours.	1945	Plea of nolo contendere.	Conspiracy to fix prices of formic acid, limit production, control channels of distribution.	Fine.	
721	E.I. duPont de Nemours.	1945	Plea of nolo contendere.	Conspiracy to control sales of muriatic acid by exchanges of product among producers and by discriminatory selling.	Fine.	
780, 802	E.I. duPont de Nemours.	1949 1947	Plea of nolo contendere. Conviction after trial.	World wide cartel agreement to allocate markets and pool patents, on titanium compounds, creating a monopoly in the United States.	Fine and injunction.	Decree includes compulsory licensing of relevant patents at reasonable royalties.
789	E.I. duPont de Nemours.	1952	Conviction after trial.	Agreement with Imperial Chemical Industries to allocate world markets, set quotas, and fix prices on wide range of products.	Injunction.	Decree includes termination of joint control of subsidiary companies and compulsory licensing of patents at reasonable royalty.
911	E.I. duPont de Nemours.	Pending.	?	Monopolizing cellophane cap and band industry and participating in agreement to exclude competitors.	?	Acquitted in lower court. Government appeal pending.

CHEMICALS (CONTINUED)

I Serial Number of Case	II Names of Defendant Companies	III Date of Final Disposition	IV Method of Decision	V Offense Charged	VI Penalty or Remedy Applied	VII Remarks
940	Union Carbide & Carbon.	Pending.	?	Conspiracy to monopolize ferrovanadium and vanadium oxide by buying control of the supply of vanadium oxide and refusing to sell it to makers of ferrovanadium. Price fixing.	?	
987 (See also Motor Vehicles)	E.I. duPont de Nemours. General Motors.	Civil Case Pending.	?	Control of General Motors by duPont and use of control to establish reciprocal purchasing arrangements and preferential prices between the two companies, excluding competition.	?	Acquitted in lower court. Government appeal pending.
MOTOR VEHICLES						
432, 566	General Motors.	1941 1952	Conviction after trial. Consent decree.	Coercion of dealers to finance cars through General Motors' subsidiary exclusively.	Fine and injunction.	
438	Chrysler Corp.	1938	Consent decree.	Coercion of dealers to finance cars exclusively through Chrysler subsidiary.	Injunction.	

144

No.	Company	Year	Plea/Outcome	Charge	Penalty	Notes
439	Ford Motor Co.	1938	Consent decree.	Coercion of dealers to finance cars exclusively through Ford subsidiary.	Injunction.	
841	General Motors.	1947	Plea of nolo contendere.	Conspiracy to fix prices of ball bearings.	Fine.	
890, 891 (See also Petroleum and Rubber)	General Motors. Standard Oil of California. Phillips Petroleum. Firestone Tire & Rubber.	1955 (civil) 1951 (Crim.)	Conviction after trial (Standard). Dismissal (others). Conviction after trial (all).	Conspiracy to monopolize sale of motor buses, tires, and gasoline, etc., to nation-wide combine of urban bus lines.	Injunction and Fines.	Standard enjoined from enforcing 3 contracts. Consent decree against bus lines. Others dismissed in civil action.
899	General Motors.	1948	Plea of nolo contendere.	Conspiracy to fix prices on clutch facings.	Fine.	
900	General Motors.	1948	Plea of nolo contendere.	Conspiracy to fix prices of friction materials.	Fine.	
901	General Motors.	1948	Plea of nolo contendere.	Conspiracy to fix prices on brake linings.	Fine.	
987 (See also Chemicals.)	General Motors. E.I. duPont de Nemours.	Civil Case Pending.	?	Control of General Motors by duPont and use of that control to establish reciprocal purchasing arrangements and preferential prices between the two companies, excluding competitors.	?	Acquitted in lower court. Government appeal pending.

DAIRY PRODUCTS

I Serial Number of Case	II Names of Defendant Companies	III Date of Final Disposition	IV Method of Decision	V Offense Charged	VI Penalty or Remedy Applied	VII Remarks
608	Sheffield Farms Co. (Subsidiary of National Dairy Products.)	1943	Plea of nolo contendere.	Conspiracy to fix whole-sale milk prices in Greater New York City on milk shipped from outside state. Coercion of distributors to adhere.	Fine.	
626	Kraft Cheese (Sub. of Nat. Dairy)	1944	Plea of nolo contendere.	Conspiracy to fix buying prices on foreign type cheese in Wisconsin.	Fine.	
641	Kraft Cheese (Sub. of Nat. Dairy)	1944	Plea of nolo contendere.	Conspiracy to fix buying prices for American and Cheddar cheese in North-ern New York.	Fine.	
642 (See also Food Distri-bution.)	Kraft Cheese (Sub. of Nat. Dairy) A. & P.	1944	Pleas of nolo contendere.	Conspiracy to fix prices to be paid for American and Cheddar cheese in Western New York.	Fines.	
927	Ewing-Von Allman Dairy (Sub. of Nat. Dairy.)	1948	Plea of nolo contendere.	Conspiracy to fix milk prices in Louisville area.	Fine.	

947	Matthews-Frechtling Dairy. (Sub. of Nat. Dairy.)	1950	Plea of nolo contendere.	Conspiracy to fix whole-sale and retail milk prices in the Cincinnati area and to withhold bottles from sellers not maintaining the prices fixed.	Fine.	
1179	Ohio Clover Leaf Dairy. (Sub. of Nat. Dairy.)	1955	Plea of nolo contendere.	Conspiracy to fix prices in Toledo area at wholesale and retail for milk, cream, and butter.	Fine.	

RUBBER

123	Firestone Tire & Rubber.	1914	Consent decree.	Conspiracy to restrain trade in horseshoes and rubber hoof pads.	Injunc-tion.	
890, 891 (See also Petro-leum and Motors.)	Firestone Tire & Rubber. General Motors. Standard Oil of California. Phillips Petroleum.	1955 (civil) 1951 (cr.)	Conviction after trial (Standard). Dismissal (others). Conviction after trial (all).	Conspiracy to monopolize sale of tires, motor buses, gasoline, etc. to nation-wide combine of urban bus lines.	Injunc-tion and Fines.	Standard enjoined from enforcing 3 contracts. Con-sent decree against bus lines. Others dismissed in civil action.
897	Goodyear Tire & Rubber. U. S. Rubber. Firestone Tire & Rubber.	1948	Plea of nolo contendere.	Conspiracy to fix prices and allocate sales of tires and tubes, and limit pro-duction of certain types.	Fines.	

I Serial Number of Case	II Names of Defendant Companies	III Date of Final Disposition	IV Method of Decision	V Offense Charged	VI or Remedy Applied	VII Remarks
956	Goodyear Tire & Rubber.	1949	Plea of nolo contendere.	Conspiracy to fix prices of leather and shoe findings, and boycott non-approved distributors.	Fine.	
967	U.S. Rubber.	1954	Consent decree.	World wide cartel on latex based on patent pool and jointly owned companies restricted to designated territories.	Injunction.	Decree includes compulsory licensing of patents at reasonable royalties, dissolution of one joint company, and assignment of management of other joint companies to a single parent without interference by others.
1012 1013 (See also Miscellaneous)	Goodyear Tire & Rubber. Montgomery Ward. Sears, Roebuck. Firestone Tire & Rubber.	1953	Pleas of nolo contendere and consent decree.	Conspiracy to channel used batteries to one company at fixed prices, and channel salvaged lead to original supplier, preventing sale to rebuilders.	Fines and injunction.	

642 (See also Dairy Products.)	Great Atlantic & Pacific Tea. Kraft Cheese (Sub. of National Dairy.)	1944	Pleas of nolo contendere.	Conspiracy to fix buying prices of American and Cheddar Cheese in Western New York.	Fines.	
611, 654	Great Atlantic & Pacific Tea.	1941	Plea of nolo contendere and consent decree.	Conspiracy to fix prices and coerce grocers to observe them under pretext of enforcing Connecticut act against sales below cost.	Fine and injunction.	
653	Great Atlantic & Pacific Tea.	1941	Consent decree.	Same as above, but for Massachusetts.	Injunction.	
666	Great Atlantic & Pacific Tea.	1941	Consent decree.	Same as above, but for Maine.	Injunction.	
674	Great Atlantic & Pacific Tea.	1941	Consent decree.	Same as above, but for Rhode Island.	Injunction.	
793, 990	Great Alantic & Pacific Tea.	1949 and 1954	Conviction after trial and consent decree.	Abuse of mass buying and selling power to restrain trade, with monopolistic tendency.	Fine and injunction.	Decree dissolves Atlantic Commission Company and forbids sale of products to outside trade unless made by A. & P.

MEAT

I Serial Number of Case	II Names of Defendant Companies	III Date of Final Disposition	IV Method of Decision	V Offense Charged	VI Penalty or Remedy Applied	VII Remarks
211	Armour. Swift.	1920	Consent decree.	Conspiracy to suppress competition in buying livestock and selling dressed meats by ownership of strategic market facilities.	Injunction.	Decree forbids holding stock in public stockyards, public cold storage plants, terminal railroads, market newspapers, handling many non-meat products, selling at retail.
318	Swift.	1926	Plea of nolo contendere.	Conspiracy to eliminate competition in terms of sale for mixed fertilizer.	Fine.	
588	Swift.	1942	Plea of nolo contendere.	Conspiracy to fix prices and divide sales territories in sale of mixed fertilizer.	Fine.	

PHOTOGRAPHIC SUPPLIES

I Serial Number of Case	II Names of Defendant Companies	III Date of Final Disposition	IV Method of Decision	V Offense Charged	VI Penalty or Remedy Applied	VII Remarks
143	Eastman Kodak.	1921	Conviction after trial.	Monopoly of photographic supplies attained by acquiring competitors.	Dissolution.	

898	Eastman Kodak.	1948	Consent decree.	Conspiracy to monopolize color cinematography by agreement to reserve patents and know-how for Technicolor.	Injunction.	Decree requires royalty-free licensing of existing patents; licensing of patents of the next 5 years at reasonable royalties; conveyance of know-how to licensees; sale of color motion picture film to all professional buyers.
1213	Eastman Kodak.	1954	Consent decree.	Tying arrangements designed to give Eastman monopoly of the development of color film.	Injunction.	Decree includes compulsory licensing of patents relating to processing of color film, provision of know-how for licensees, temporary cancellation of resale price controls under state laws; and eventual partial divestiture if needed to create alternative processors.

NON-FERROUS METALS

I Serial of Case Number	II Names of Companies	III Date of Final Disposition	IV Method of Decision	V Offense Charged	VI Penalty or Remedy Applied	VII Remarks
423	Aluminum Co. of America.	1950	Conviction after trial.	Monopolizing virgin aluminum.	Partial divestiture and compulsory sale of components.	Establishment of new suppliers during World War II made dissolution unnecessary.
580 581 582 698	Aluminum Co. of America.	1942	Pleas of nolo contendere in first three cases. Consent decree in last.	Monopoly of magnesium, based upon pooled patents, accompanied by limitation of output, price fixing, and measures to prevent new competition.	Fines and injunction.	Decree includes royalty-free compulsory licensing for fabrication patents and temporarily for production patents.
849	International Nickel of Canada.	1948	Consent decree.	Conspiracy to monopolize nickel and nickel products, limit world production, fix world prices, and allocate sales.	Injunction.	Decree requires sale of basic nickel raw materials to producers of nickel rolling mill products for 20 years.

STEEL

378	Bethlehem Steel.	1931	Consent decree.	Conspiracy to fix prices of bolts, nuts, and rivets, and maintain a black list of customers.	Injunction.	Decree includes compulsory licensing of relevant patents at reasonable royalties.
810,	Bethlehem Steel.	1945	Pleas of nolo contendere.	Conspiracy to fix prices of stainless steel and exchange advance information about bids to government.	Fines and injunction.	
815	American Rolling Mill.	1948	Consent decree.			

TOBACCO

49	American Tobacco. (Predecessor of present company.)	1911	Conviction after trial.	Monopoly attained by local price cutting to destroy competitors and buying out competitors.	Dissolution.	
547	American Tobacco. Liggett & Myers Tobacco. R.J. Reynolds Tobacco.	1946	Conviction after trial.	Conspiracy to monopolize leaf buying and cigarette manufacture; involved fixing buying prices for leaf, fixing cigarette prices, and efforts to destroy independent competitors.	Fines.	

SOAP PRODUCTS

I Serial Number of Case	II Names of Defendant Companies	III Date of Final Disposition	IV Method of Decision	V Offense Charged	VI Penalty or Remedy Applied	VII Remarks
748	Proctor & Gamble.	1942	Plea of nolo contendere.	Conspiracy to fix prices on soap products.	Fine.	
1150	Proctor & Gamble.	Civil Case Pending.	?	Conspiracy to fix prices on soap and synthetic detergents, fix buying prices of raw materials, and monopolize manufacture by acquisition of competitors and exchange of patents.	?	

MISCELLANEOUS

I Serial Number of Case	II Names of Defendant Companies	III Date of Final Disposition	IV Method of Decision	V Offense Charged	VI Penalty or Remedy Applied	VII Remarks
115	International Harvester.	1918	Conviction after trial.	Monopoly of agricultural machinery, attained by combining competitors.	Dissolution.	
192	International Paper.	1917	Consent decree.	Conspiracy to raise newsprint prices by various means, including limitations of production.	Injunction.	As part of remedy, defendants agreed that during World War I they would sell newsprints at prices set by a government agency.

No.	Company	Case	Charge	Disposition
1012 1013	Mongomery Ward. Sears, Roebuck. (See also Rubber) Goodyear Tire & Rubber. Firestone Tire & Rubber.	1953	Conspiracy to channel used batteries to one company at fixed prices and channel salvaged lead to original supplier, preventing sale to rebuilders.	Pleas of nolo contendere and consent decree. / Fines and injunction.
1203	United Fruit.	Civil Case Pending.	Conspiracy to monopolize the banana trade and monopoly thereof, by acquiring competitors, allocating business, preempting suitable land and transportation facilities, and reducing prices to destroy competition.	? / ?
1225	Schenley Industries Distillers Distributing Corp. (Sub. of Distillers Corp.—Seagrams, Ltd.) Joseph E. Seagram & Sons. (Sub. of Distillers Corp.—Seagrams, Ltd.)	Criminal Case Pending.	Participation in conspiracy, enforced by boycotts, to raise and fix liquor prices in Maryland by use of resale price contracts.	? / ?

155

In Table II the first column contains the Federal Trade Commission's docket number, which identifies the case in official files. Column two contains the names of those defendants in the case that were among the largest fifty industrial companies. Column three states what part of the statutes was violated and column four the year in which the case was decided, after any appeals which may have taken place. Column five shows whether the Commission's order was the result of a contested decision or was entered with the consent of the defendant. Column six states the nature of the offense.[1] Column seven contains such remarks as appear to be needed to indicate the significance of the proceedings.

---

[1] Where a consent order is entered, the Commission's findings of fact are usually limited and sometimes cover nothing more than the facts showing that the Commission had jurisdiction; the defendant does not formally admit guilt; and the nature of the offense can be determined only from the limited findings, the complaint which instituted the case, and the Commission's order. Inferences thus grounded are sometimes difficult. In Docket 5508, for example, the Commission's complaint charged a conspiracy to fix prices by use of a basing point system supplemented by lists of agreed extra charges and deductions. The Commission's findings cover the activities mentioned, but include no formal finding that there was a conspiracy; instead they state that these activities tended to suppress competition. The Commission's order forbids the activities when part of a planned common course of action. Presumably the ambiguity of the findings is the result of a comprise, in which language was chosen which, to the Commission's attorneys, is the equivalent of a finding of conspiracy but to the defense attorneys falls short of any such finding. The case has been treated here as one of conspiracy because, though the findings are ambiguous, the complaint and the order clearly have to do with conspiracy.

TABLE II: FEDERAL TRADE COMMISSION CASES (INCLUDING CASES PENDING)

PETROLEUM

I Docket	II Names of Defendant Companies	III Statutes and Section	V Date of Final Disposition	IV Method of Decision	VI Offense Charged	VII Remarks
85 133	Standard Oil (Ind.)	Clayton 3 FTCA 5	1920	Stipulation of facts.	Contracting to lease pumps and tanks to dealers below cost on condition rivals' products not handled.	Two of eight paralled cases against different companies, of which six were dismissed on appeal. These were not appealed.
1038	Gulf Refining (Sub. of Gulf Oil) Texas Co.	FTCA 5	1924	Trial and order.	Participation in agreement to fix prices of gasoline in Tampa, Florida, by refusing to supply dealers who did not comply.	
4389	Standard Oil (Ind.)	Clayton 2	Pending	Trial and order.	Price discrimination on gasoline in Detroit.	First order set aside by Supreme Court because Commission had refused to consider whether competition had been met in good faith. Second order 1953, based on lack of good faith, has been appealed.

Petroleum (Continued)

I Docket	II Names of Defendant Companies	III Statutes and Section	IV Date of Final Disposition	V Method of Decision	VI Offense Charged	VII Remarks
4390	Gulf Oil.	Clayton 2	Pending.	?	Discrimination in price of gasoline sold to Firestone and Goodrich in Detroit.	
4391	Texas Co.	Clayton 2	Pending.	?	Discrimination in price of gasoline sold to Firestone and Goodrich in Detroit.	
5794	Standard Oil (N. J.) Standard Oil (Ind.) Standard Oil of Calif.	Clayton 2 FTCA 5	1951	Consent order.	Inducing price discriminations on tires, batteries, and automobile parts and accessories by purchase through a jointly owned buying agency.	
					Steel	
760	U.S. Steel.	Clayton 2 FTCA 5	1948	Trial and order.	Discrimination in price of steel products thru operation of a basing point system.	The famous Pittsburgh plus case. Commission's order 1924. Appealed in 1938. Consent decree of affirmance, 1948.

Docket	Company	Statute	Year	Proceeding	Charge	Disposition
2741	Bethlehem Steel. Jones & Laughlin Steel. Republic Steel. Youngstown Sheet and Tube.	FTCA 5	1936	Material facts admitted.	Agreement not to sell second quality tin plate as such quality but to require buyers of first quality to accept up to 25% of seconds; and to cut unsold seconds into sizes not suited to can manufacture.	
4452 (See also Electrical)	Republic Steel. Youngstown Sheet and Tube. General Electric.	FTCA 5	1949	Trial and order.	Conspiracy to fix prices of rigid steel conduit by use of a basing point system, uniform contracts, trade discounts collectively considered, and agreed classifications of customers.	Order 1944. Second count charging parallel action but not conspiracy appealed and affirmed, 1949.
5508	U.S. Steel. Bethlehem Steel. Republic Steel. Jones & Laughlin Steel. Armco Steel (name formerly American Rolling Mill.) National Steel. Youngstown Sheet & Tube.	FTCA 5	1951	Consent order.	Joint use of basing point system and lists of extras and deductions with tendency to suppress competition.	
6078	U.S. Steel. Republic Steel. Jones & Laughlin Steel.	FTCA 5	1955	Consent order.	Conspiracy to fix prices on steel drums through use of basing point system, extra lists, and exchange of pricing factors.	Charge was price fixing conspiracy, and order prohibits planned common course of action.

I Docket	II Names of Defendant Companies	III Statutes and Section	IV Date of Final Disposition	V Method of Decision	VI Offense Charged	VII Remarks
6156	U.S. Steel.	FTCA 5	Pending.	?	Participation in conspiracy to give one steel scrap broker a monopoly by exclusive arrangements with him as to purchase and sale of scrap and by coercing fabricators and railroads to give him preference in sale of scrap.	
6225	Republic Steel.	FTCA 5	1954	Consent order.	Participation in conspiracy to fix prices on metal rain goods (i.e., funnels, elbows, etc.) by use of zone pricing system, exchange of price lists, classification of customers and correspondence about deviations from standard terms.	

RUBBER

I Docket	II Names of Defendant Companies	III Statutes and Section	IV Date of Final Disposition	V Method of Decision	VI Offense Charged	VII Remarks
2354	Goodyear Tire & Rubber.	FTCA 5	1935	Consent order.	Participation in agreement to fix prices and resale prices of mechanical rubber goods. Refusal to supply noncompliers.	

No.	Company	Act	Year	Order	Description
2565	U.S. Rubber. (See also Non-Ferrous & Electrical) General Electric. Anaconda Wire & Cable (Sub. of Anaconda). Kennecott Wire & Cable (Sub. of Kennecott)	FTCA 5	1936	Consent order.	Conspiracy to fix prices on power cable and rubber covered building wire.
3685	U.S. Rubber	Clayton 2	1939	Consent order.	Discrimination in price of tires on behalf of mail-order houses and chain stores, in private brand sales and otherwise.
4972	U.S. Rubber	Clayton 2	1950	Stipulation of facts.	Discrimination in price of waterproof rubber footwear and canvas footwear.
5448	Goodyear Tire & Rubber. U.S. Rubber.	FTCA 5	1948	Stipulation of facts.	Participation in conspiracy to fix prices and resale prices on rubber heels and soles.
5635	Goodyear Tire & Rubber. (See also U.S. Rubber. Motors) General Motors.	FTCA 5	1951	Stipulation of facts.	Participation in agreement by which members of associations of bicycle parts makers and jobbers would deal only with each other, cutting off mail order houses, other independent distributors, and independent suppliers.

I	II	III	IV	V	VI	VII
Docket	Names of Defendant Companies	Statutes and Section	Date of Final Disposition	Method of Decision	Offense Charged	Remarks
6044	Goodyear Tire & Rubber.	Clayton 2	1953	Consent order.	Discrimination in prices of shoe products through cumulative annual volume discounts up to 6.5% on $100,000 or over.	

MOTORS

I	II	III	IV	V	VI	VII
3152	General Motors.	FTCA 5 Clayton 3	1942	Trial and order.	Coercion of dealers to stock only automobile parts and accessories distributed by General Motors and to accept shipments not ordered.	
5620	General Motors.	Clayton 2 Clayton 3	1953	Trial and order.	Discrimination in prices of AC spark plugs, and use of rebates as inducement for exclusive dealing agreements.	

Docket	Company	Law	Year	Action	Charge	Remarks
5635	General Motors. (See also Rubber.)Goodyear Tire & Rubber.U.S. Rubber.	FTCA 5	1951	Consent order.	Participation in agreement by which members of association of bicycle parts makers and jobbers would deal only with each other, cutting off mail order houses, other independent distributors, and independent suppliers.	

ELECTRICAL

Docket	Company	Law	Year	Action	Charge	Remarks
2565	General Electric. Anaconda Wire & Cable (Sub. of Anaconda) and Kennecott Wire & Cable (Sub. of Kennecott) U.S. Rubber. (See also Rubber Anaconda Non-Ferrous	FTCA 5	1936	Consent order.	Conspiracy to fix prices on power cable, and rubber covered building wire.	Civil penalties for violation of order were imposed on General Electric and Anaconda Wire & Cable in 1947.
2941	General Electric. Westinghouse Electric	FTCA 2	1937	Consent order.	Conspiracy to fix prices on turbine generators, including agreement on bids to be submitted.	
4452	General Electric. (See also Steel) Republic Steel. Youngstown Sheet & Tube.	FTCA 5	1949	Trial and order.	Conspiracy to fix prices of rigid steel conduit by use of basing point system, uniform contracts, trade discounts collectively considered, and agreed classifications of customers.	Second count charging paralleled action but not conspiracy, appealed and affirmed, 1949.

Non-Ferrous

Docket (I)	Names of Defendant Companies (II)	Statutes and Section (III)	Date of Final Disposition (IV)	Method of Decision (V)	Offense Charged (VI)	Remarks (VII)
248	Aluminum Co. of America.	Clayton 7	1921	Trial and order.	Joint ownership of stock in competing aluminum rolling mill.	Ordered to divest self of stock.
5253	Anaconda Copper.	FTCA 5 Clayton 2	Pending	Trial and order.	Participation in price agreement on lead pigments involving zone pricing system set up under cloak of NRA code and continued thereafter. Discrimination in zone differentials.	1953 order has been appealed.
2565	Anaconda Wire & Cable (Sub. of Anaconda) Kennecott Wire & Cable (Sub. of Kennecott) U.S. Rubber. General Electric (See also Rubber and Electrical)	FTCA 5	1936	Consent order.	Conspiracy to fix prices on power cable and rubber covered building wire.	Civil penalties for violation of order were imposed on Anaconda Wire & Cable and General Electric in 1947.

Liquor

Docket (I)	Names of Defendant Companies (II)	Statutes and Section (III)	Date of Final Disposition (IV)	Method of Decision (V)	Offense Charged (VI)	Remarks (VII)
2988	Seagram Distillers (Sub. of Distiller Corp.-Seagram)	FTCA 5	1938	Material allegations admitted.	Fixing resale prices in the District of Columbia.	

2990	Schenley Industries	FTCA 5	1938	Material allegations admitted.	Fixing resale prices in the District of Columbia.
4093	Schenley Industries	FTCA 5	1940	Material facts admitted.	Participation in conspiracy to fix prices of liquor, coerce noncompliers, and withhold liquor from cooperative buying associations, small jobbers and other distributors classed as irregular.
6048	Schenley Industries	FTCA 5	1954	Consent settlement.	Participation with its subsidiaries in conspiracy to fix prices and resale prices of liquor in conference with liquor dealers and their representatives.

DAIRY PRODUCTS

4071	Kraft-Phenix Cheese (Sub. of National Dairy.)	FTCA 5	1940	Stipulation of facts.	Conspiracy to fix prices of Swiss and Limburger cheese in Wisconsin.
4647	Sheffield Farms (Sub. of National Dairy.)	FTCA 5	1948	Trial and order.	Dominating an association of milk producers to obtain buying advantages over competitors and impair bargaining power of members.

I Docket	II Names of Defendant Companies	III Statutes and Section	IV Date of Final Disposition	V Method of Decision	VI Offense Charged	VII Remarks
6175	National Dairy and various subsidiaries.	FTCA 5	Pending.	?	Exclusion of competitors by supplying fixtures, facilities, services, and loans to retail dealers below cost and granting rebates and discounts on condition dealers will cease to carry competitors' products.	

CHEMICALS

I Docket	II Names of Defendant Companies	III Statutes and Section	IV Date of Final Disposition	V Method of Decision	VI Offense Charged	VII Remarks
4145	E.I. duPont de Nemours.	FTCA 5	1942	Stipulation of Facts.	Participation in conspiracy to fix prices of agricultural insecticides and fungicides, including prices in public bids, and agreement as to dealers to be recognized.	
5979	E.I. duPont de Nemours.	FTCA 5	1952	Consent settlement.	Participation in conspiracy to monopolize trade in surgical equipment sold to physicians and hospitals. Conspiracy included refusal to sell to dealers not approved by association, limiting number of dealers, reciprocal preferences, resale price maintenance.	

Film

977	Eastman Kodak	FTCA 5	1927	Stipulation of facts.	Effort to maintain monopoly of film for moving pictures by purchase of film-development laboratories and agreement not to operate them if association of developers would buy only film made in United States.	1924 order affirmed on appeal.
4322	Eastman Kodak	FTCA 5	1947	Trial and order.	Fixing resale prices on Kodachrome and magazine film which was not in free and open competition with other products of like grade and quality.	1944 order affirmed on appeal.

Miscellaneous

231	Armour	FTCA 5	1919	Stipulation of facts.	Organizing and operating a bogus independent fertilizer company.	
886	American Tobacco	FTCA 5	1927	Trial and order.	Participation in conspiracy of wholesale tobacco dealers to fix prices by refusing to supply price cutters.	1924 order affirmed on appeal.
3031	Atlantic & Pacific Tea	Clayton 2	1940	Trial and order.	Exacting discounts from sellers in lieu of brokerage.	1938 order affirmed on appeal.

MISCELLANEOUS (CONTINUED)

I Docket	II Names of Defendant Companies	III Statutes and Section	IV Date of Final Disposition	V Method of Decision	VI Offense Charged	VII Remarks
3760	International Paper	FTCA 5	1949	Trial and order.	Participation in agreement on delivered price zones and price differentials for book paper by continuing NRA code.	1945 order affirmed on appeal.
3783	Proctor & Gamble Distributing (Sub. of Proctor & Gamble)	Clayton 2	1945	Trial and order.	Participation in grant of brokerage to a buyers' organization.	1943 order affirmed on appeal.

INDEX

Achnacarry agreement, 19
Acid, chromic, 60, 142
Acid, formic, 60, 143
Acid, muriatic, 60, 143
Acid, sulfuric, 60, 142
AC Spark Plug Co., 94
Adams, Walter, 117
Agreements, 3, 12, 13, 37, 38, 52-54, 59-63, 65-66, 90, 97, 102, 111, 112, 115-
    117, 126-130, 131, 135-155, 156, 157, 159-161, 163-168
Agricultural price supports, 7
Airplanes, 99
Allied Chemical & Dye Corp., 141, 142
Allocation of markets, 19, 53, 60, 67, 76, 97, 111, 116, 126-127, 130, 136,
    137, 138, 139, 140, 142, 143, 147, 148, 152, 155
Aluminum, 33, 36, 62, 85, 95, 102, 109, 152, 164
Aluminum Company of America, 9, 36, 85, 152, 164
American Brass Co., 46-47
American Can Co., 22
American Magnesium Corp., 36
American Rolling Mill Co.—see Armco Steel Co.
American Telephone and Telegraph Co., 141
American Tobacco Co., 62, 66, 153, 167
Anaconda Copper Mining Co., 58, 63, 66, 95, 161, 163, 164
Anaconda Wire and Cable Co., 161, 163, 164
Anglo-American Council on Productivity, 91
Anti-Merger Act, 123-124
Antitrust laws
    bigness as an element in violating, 21-23, 26
    case-by-case procedure, 21, 113-114
    cases involving big companies, 9-10, 54-68, 133-168
    influence toward competition, 74-75, 100
    objectives of, 5
    performance tests not suited to, 113-118, 131
    principal expression of competitive policy, 20-21, 114, 130
    Report of Attorney General's Committee on, 9
Armco Steel Corp., 49, 153, 159
Armour and Co., 150, 167
Arnold, Thurman, 46-47
Atlantic and Pacific Tea Co., 21, 65, 82, 146, 149, 167
Atlantic Commission Co., 149
Atlantic Refining Co., 63, 67
Attorney General's National Committee to Study the Antitrust Laws,
    Report, 9

Ball bearings, 61, 145
Bananas, 63, 155
Basing-point system, 65, 158, 159, 163
Batteries, 63, 66, 148, 155, 158
Berle, Adolf A., 13, 18-19, 106, 119
Beryllium, 46-47
Bethlehem Steel Corp., 49, 65, 153, 159
Bicycle parts, 66, 161, 163
Big companies
    conduct checked by
        antitrust laws, 21-23
        big government, 18
        corporate conscience, 19
        countervailing power, 18-20
        desire to grow, 75-76
        internal conflicts, 17, 101-102
    competitive pressures upon, 72-76, 98-99
    defenses of, 15-21, 23, 70, 97-102
    defined, 38-41
    extent of competition by
        in cyclical pricing, 79-81
        in long-run pricing, 81-86
        in short-run pricing, 77-79
        in efficiency, 91-95, 102, 107-108
        in quality, 86-88, 90-91
        in research, 88-91, 102, 107-108
        with small companies, 76-77
        summarized, 102-103, 107
    instability of, 17-18, 100-101
    involvement in antitrust cases, 54-68, 135-168
    methods of growth, 75-76
    numbers, 40-41
    related to
        agreements, 12-13, 52-54, 126-130, 131
        fewness, 12-13
        good economic performance, 70-71, 77-97
        opportunity for new ventures, 11, 12, 13
        small business, 10-11, 12, 13, 24, 76-77
    responsiveness to market forces, 11-12, 13
    sources of power, 11, 28, 29-31, 36-38, 38-54, 87-90, 93-94, 99-100, 102, 112-113, 129-130, 132
        buying advantages, 43, 93-94, 100, 112
        capacity to litigate, 50-51
        collusion, 53-54
        control of distribution, 47-48
        control of patents, 50-52, 89-90, 99, 129-130
        diversification, 11, 44-45
        monopoly, 29-31
        oligopoly, 36-38

one-way respect, 46
political influence, 49-50
reciprocal buying, 53
sales effort, 87-88, 102
spending power, 48-49
squeezes, 48, 112
transfer of risks, 44, 48
vertical integration, 11, 43-44, 112-113
standards for policy toward
    as to fixed limits on bigness, 108-110
    as to information, 119-122
    as to joint action, 126-130
    as to mergers, 122-124
    as to voluntary divestiture, 124-126
structurally inconsistent with competition, 10-13
Biscuits and crackers, 109
Blair, John, 78
Blacklist—see boycott
Bogus independent, 65
Bolts, nuts, and rivets, 153
Book paper, 168—see also newsprint, paper
Boom—see business cycle
Boycott, 2, 22, 148, 153, 155
Brake linings, 62, 145
Brokerage, 66, 168
Business cycle, 7, 72, 79-81, 98, 117
Butter, 147—see also cheese, cream, milk

Cable, high tension, 60, 140
Canvas footwear, 161
Celler, Emanuel, 32, 123
Cellophane, 61, 96-97, 143
Chain stores, 24, 62
Champion Spark Plug Co., 94
Chance Vought Aircraft, Inc., 125
Checks and balances, 1, 2, 105
Cheese, 61, 62, 146, 149, 165—see also butter, cream, milk
Chemicals, generally, 89, 102, 127, 141-144, 166—see also acid, cellophane,
    dyestuffs, explosives, insecticides, nitrogen, nylon, orlon, synthetic
    fibers, petrochemicals, plastics, photographic supplies, titanium, vana-
    dium
Chrysler Corp., 144
Cigarettes, 33, 62, 96, 102, 153—see also tobacco
Clayton Act, 56, 63, 64—see also Robinson-Patman Act
Clutch facings, 61, 145
Coercion, 61, 62, 65-67, 77, 144, 145, 149, 155, 157, 160, 162, 167
Color cinematography, 62, 151—see also photographic supplies
Color film—see photographic supplies

Columbia Steel Co., 9
Commerce Clearing House, 55
Commerce, Secretary of, 32
Competition
 environment for big companies, 73-74
 fostered by
  antitrust laws, 20-21, 74-75
  "creative destruction," 16-17, 99
  environmental change, 72-73, 98-99, 101
  long-run thinking, 17
  pressures within enterprise, 17, 101-102
 kinds of
  among big companies, 77-95, 100, 102-103
   in efficiency, 91-95
   in price, 77-86
   in quality, 86-88, 91
   in research, 88-91
  between big and little, 76-77, 111, 112
  of substitutes, 34-35, 95-97
 political concept of, 1-4, 70, 100, 105, 115, 131
 related to
  conservation, 7, 8
  countervailing power, 18, 19-20, 100
  desire to grow, 75-76, 113
  diversification, 44-45, 111-112
  economic performance, 5-9, 16, 70-72, 114-118
  freedom, 3-4
  labor standards, 7, 8
  mergers, 122-124
  military preparedness, 7
  oligopoly, 31-38
  stability, 7, 8
  vertical integration, 112-113
 structurally inconsistent with bigness, 10-13
 supplemented by control, 6-8, 105-106
Concentration
 curbs upon abuse of, 15-20, 110-113, 119-132
 danger in increase, 106-107
 evidence of monopoly, 21-22
 extent of, 32-36, 39-40, 106
 information needed about, 119-120
 political objections to, 1, 3, 9-10
 related to
  desire to grow, 113
  price inflexibility, 78-79
 trend of, 13-14, 106-107
 weakness in figures about, 34-36
Conduit, rigid steel, 65, 66, 159, 163

Congress, 118, 124
Conservation, 7, 8
Control of distributive channels, 47-48, 66, 136, 142, 143, 144, 145, 148, 155, 160, 161, 162, 163, 165, 166
Copper, 58-59, 95
Cork, 33
Corn products, 33, 35
Cost accounting, 41, 92
Cotton, 95
"Creative destruction," 16-17, 19, 20, 23, 99
Cox, Hugh, 46-47
Cream, 147—see also butter, cheese, milk
Crude oil, 137—see also petroleum

Dairy products—see butter, cheese, cream, milk
Detergents, 62, 154
Distillers Corp.-Seagram, Ltd., 57, 67, 155, 164
Distillers Distributing Corp., 57, 155
Diversification, 11-12, 44-45, 95, 97, 111-112, 132
Douglas, Mr. Justice, 9
Dow Chemical Co., 36
Drop-out fuse cutouts, 60, 139
DuPont de Nemours Co., E. I., 22, 60-61, 66, 93, 96-97, 141-144, 145, 166
Dyestuffs, 60, 62, 142

Eastman Kodak Co., 67, 150, 151, 167
Edwards, Corwin D., 42, 101, 110, 129
Efficiency, 5, 44, 91-95, 107-108
Electric Auto-Lite Co., 94
Electric equipment generally, 60, 65-66, 137-141, 163—see also cable, conduit, drop-out fuse cutouts, electric home appliances, electric lamps, electric refrigerators, power cable, switches, street lighting equipment, telephone equipment
Electric home appliances, 45-46
Electric lamps, 33, 60, 137, 138, 139
    glass bulbs, 138
    tubing, 138
Electric refrigerators, 85
Employment Act of 1946, 8
Ewing-Von Allman Dairy Co., 146
Exclusion from markets, 60, 66, 67, 107, 135-139, 142-144, 147-148, 151-155, 157, 160-163, 165-167
Exclusive dealing, 22, 47-48, 61, 62, 64, 67, 136, 141, 144-145, 157, 160, 161, 162, 163, 166
Explosives, 60, 141

Fairless, Benjamin, 80
Farm machinery, 62, 154

Federal Trade Commission, 13, 22, 32, 40, 49, 55-57, 58, 64, 65, 66-67, 94, 106, 119, 124, 128, 156, 157-168
Federal Trade Commission Act, 56, 64
Ferrovanadium—see vanadium
Fertilizer, mixed, 62, 150, 167
Film—see photographic supplies
Firestone Tire and Rubber Co., 137, 145, 147, 148
Food distribution, 149
Ford Motor Co., 82, 93, 120, 145
Fortune magazine, 40
Freedom, 1-2, 3-4, 9, 20
Friction materials, 61, 145
Fullbright, Senator, 80
Full-line forcing, 48

Galbraith, Kenneth, 18-20, 100
Gasoline, 59, 65, 66, 135-137, 145, 147, 157-158—see also petroleum
General Electric Co., 45, 60, 65, 66, 84, 137-141, 159, 161, 163, 164
General Motors Corp., 45, 61, 65, 66, 67, 84, 93, 94, 95, 144, 145, 161, 162, 163
Glass bottles, 116-117
Glass, flat, 33
Goodyear Tire and Rubber Co., 66, 147, 148, 155, 160-163
Great Atlantic and Pacific Tea Co.—see Atlantic and Pacific Tea Co.
Gulf Oil Co., 66, 137, 157, 158
Gulf Refining Co., 157
Gypsum products, 33
Hand, Learned, 9
Hard-surfaced floor coverings, 33
Hartford-Empire Co., 116
Horseshoes, 147
House Judiciary Committee, subcommittee on study of monopoly, 32, 49

Imperial Chemical Industries, 90, 127, 143
Inequality, 3, 10-11, 12
Innovation, 5, 11, 16-17, 72-73, 75, 86-90, 95, 98-99, 102, 107-108
Insecticides, 66, 166
Interlocks, personal, 63, 128-129
Internal Revenue Service, 40
International Harvester Co., 154
International Nickel Co. of Canada, 152
International Paper Co., 66, 154, 168
Iron Ore, 48-49

Joint ownership of facilities, 53, 127, 138, 148, 150, 164
Jones and Laughlin Steel Corp., 63, 65, 159
Jones, Eliot, 92
Justice, Department of, 55, 63, 67, 124, 133, 135

Kaplan, A. D. H., 14, 17-18, 19, 20, 55, 100-102
Kefauver, Estes, 123
Kennecott Copper Corp., 58, 63, 161, 163, 164
Kennecott Wire and Cable Co., 161, 163, 164
Kodachrome—see photographic supplies
Kraft Cheese Co., 61, 146, 149, 165
Kraft-Phenix Cheese Corp.—see Kraft Cheese Co.

Labor legislation, 7, 117
Labor standards, 7, 8, 117
Labor unions, 4, 18, 100, 102
Latex, 61, 148
Lead, 66, 148, 155, 164
Leases of machinery, 22
Leasing below cost, 64, 157—see also sale below cost, supplying facilities
    below cost
Leather and shoe findings, 148
Lever Brothers, 120
Liggett and Myers Tobacco Co., 153
Lilienthal, David, 18, 24
Limits upon bigness, 24-25, 108-110
Liquor, 63, 66, 155, 164-165
Livestock, 62, 150
Long-term contracts, 11, 22

Magnesium, 36, 152
M. A. Hanna Co., 49
Mail-order houses, 63, 155
Matches, 33
Matthews-Frechtling Dairy Co., 147
Means, Gardiner, 13, 106, 119
Meat, 61-62, 150
Mechanical rubber goods, 66, 160
Mergers, 57, 76, 101, 102, 122-124, 131
Metal rain goods, 65
Migration, 72
Milk, 61, 67, 102, 108, 146, 147, 165, 166—see also butter, cheese, cream
Minute Maid Corp., 99
Mission on Japanese Combines, 41
Monopoly
    aluminum industry, 102
    antitrust cases involving, 59-63, 64-67, 135-168
    defined, 29
    circumstances fostering, 21, 29-31, 42
    curbs upon, 16-18, 72-76
    economic characteristics of, 8
    political objections to, 2-4, 9-10
    prevalence of, 31

    public control of, 7-8, 105, 108, 111-113
    related to
      bigness, 21-22, 29-31, 131-132
        conservation, 8
        "creative destruction," 17, 19, 23
        kind and number of competitors, 30
        labor standards, 8
        military preparedness, 8
        price reductions, 83
        stability, 8
        vertical integration, 112
    small companies possessing, 30
    telephone industry, 6
Monopsony, 29
Montgomery Ward and Co., 148, 155
Morton Salt Co., 22
Motion picture film—see photographic supplies
Motor buses, 137, 145, 147—see also motor vehicles
Motor vehicles, 34, 61, 62, 85-86, 88, 90, 93-94, 102, 109, 137, 144-145, 147—
    see also motor buses, motor vehicle parts
Motor vehicle parts, 66, 67, 158, 162—see also batteries, brake linings, clutch
    facings, friction materials, spark plugs
Mueller, Willard F., 97
Muller, Charlotte F., 85

National Association of Manufacturers, 16, 29
National Bureau of Economic Research, 42
National Dairy Products Co., 57, 61, 64, 67, 146, 147, 149, 165, 166
National Recovery Administration, 81, 94
National Resources Committee, 78
National Steel Corp., 49, 63, 159
Neal, Alfred C., 78
Newsprint paper, 62, 154—see also book paper, paper
New York Great Atlantic and Pacific Tea Co.—see Atlantic and Pacific
    Tea Co.
Nickel, 62, 152
Nitrogen, 60, 62, 141
Nylon, 95—see also synthetic fibers

Ohio Clover Leaf Dairy, 147
Oil—see petroleum
Oligopoly, 31-38, 111
Orlon, 95—see also synthetic fibers
Osborn, Richards C., 91

Paper, 66—see also book paper, newsprint
Patents, 30, 35, 50-52, 89-90, 99, 102, 129-130
    in antitrust cases, 116, 136, 138, 139, 140, 143, 148, 151, 152, 154

Performance tests, 113-118
Petrochemicals, 127
Petroleum, 19, 36, 59-60, 64, 108, 127, 135-137, 157-158—see also crude oil, gasoline, petrochemicals
Phillips Petroleum Co., 135, 137, 145, 147
Photographic supplies, 62, 67, 150, 151, 167—see also color cinematography
Plastics, 95
Population growth, 72
Power
    checks upon, among big companies, 15-20
    countervailing, 18, 19-20, 100
    measurement of, 27
    prevalence of illegal use, 54-68, 133-168
    related to
        bigness, 28-54, 87-88, 93-95, 100-101, 107-108, 111-113, 129-130, 132
        democracy, 1-4, 27-29
        environmental change, 72-73
    Zaibatsu-type, 41-42
Power cable, 66, 161, 163, 164
Preemption of
    markets, 11, 21-22, 123, 136, 141, 150, 157, 160, 161, 162, 163, 166, 167
    supplies, 11, 21, 48-49, 123, 144, 155, 160
Preferential treatment, 43, 48—see also price discrimination
President's Committee of Industrial Analysis, 81
Price discrimination, 22, 43, 56, 65, 66, 78-79, 85, 93, 100, 112, 135, 144, 145, 157, 158, 161, 162, 164, 167, 168—see also preferential treatment
Price fixing, 59-62, 65-66, 115-117, 135-150, 152-155, 157, 159-161, 163-168
Price leadership, 38, 46-47, 77
Prices, generally, 2, 115-117
    flexibility and inflexibility, 5-6, 19, 78-81
    policies toward
        in business cycle, 79-81
        in long run, 81-86
        in short run, 77-79
    reductions under monopoly, 83, 85
    related to
        costs, 5, 82-83
        prices of raw materials, 78
        prices of substitutes, 96-97
        variations in quality, 85
        volume of sales, 16, 79-81, 82-86
    selective price cutting, 45, 135, 155
    under oligopoly, 37-38
Procter and Gamble Co., 154, 168
Procter and Gamble Distributing Co., 168
Public policy as to
    collusion, 126-130, 131
    fixed limits on bigness, 108-110

information about big companies, 119-122, 130-131
joint subsidiaries, 127-128, 131
joint trade-marks, 129, 131
mergers, 122-124, 131
personal interlocks, 128-129, 131
stock ownership in other corporations, 128, 131
technological interchange, 127, 129-130, 131
voluntary divestiture, 124-126, 131

Quality, 5, 16, 65, 85-88, 90-91, 102, 103
Quinn, T. K., 45

Radio communication, 60, 138
Radio Corporation of America, 138
Randall, H. L., 46-47
Reciprocal buying, 53
Republic Steel Corporation, 49, 63, 65, 159, 160, 163
Resale price maintenance, 8, 24, 48, 67, 155, 160, 161, 164, 165, 166, 167
Restriction of production or sale, 5, 67, 137, 138, 139, 141, 142, 143, 147, 152, 154
Reynolds Tobacco Co., R. J., 153
Riverside Metal Co., 46-47
Robinson-Patman Act, 22—see also Clayton Act
Rubber, generally, 65, 66, 147-148, 160-161—see also latex, mechanical rubber goods, canvas footwear, rubber footwear, rubber heels and soles, rubber hoof pads, power cable, rubber-covered building wire, tires, shoe products, leather and shoe findings
Rubber footwear, 33, 161—see also shoe products
Rubber heels and soles, 66, 161—see also shoe products
Rubber hoof pads, 147
Rubber-covered building wire, 66, 161, 163, 164
Rule of reason, 114

Sale below cost, 24, 94—see also leasing below cost, supplying facilities below cost
Sales effort, 87-88, 102
Salt, 33
Schenley Industries, 57, 67, 155, 165
Schumpeter, Joseph, 16, 19, 20, 23, 99
Scrap (steel), 65-66, 160
Seagram-Distillers Corp., 164
Seagram & Sons, Inc., Joseph E., 155
Sears, Roebuck and Co., 148, 155
Securities and Exchange Commission, 40
Seltzer, Lawrence H., 86
Sewing machines, 33
Sheffield Farms Co., 146, 165
Shell Oil Co., 136, 137

Sherman Act, 9, 57, 59, 60, 63, 64, 65, 66, 67
Sherman, John, Senator, 10
Shoe products (rubber), 162—see also rubber footwear, rubber heels and soles
Silk, 95
Sinclair Oil Co., 135
Small business, 10, 11, 12, 14, 19, 21, 24, 28, 30, 37, 38, 41, 43-44, 45-52, 67, 74, 76-77, 82, 84, 87, 88-89, 91-92, 95, 99, 100, 101, 107, 111, 112, 116-117, 120-121
Small business agencies of government, 24, 50
Soap, 33, 62, 108, 154
Socony-Vacuum Oil Co., 135, 137
Spark plugs, 65, 93-94, 162—see also motor vehicle parts
Stability, 7, 8, 17, 44
Standard contract forms, 38 39, 48
Standard Oil Co. of California, 22, 66, 135, 136, 137, 145, 147, 158
Standard Oil Co. (Indiana), 66, 135, 157, 158
Standard Oil Co. (N. J.), 57, 66, 135, 136, 137, 158
Standard Oil Co. of New Jersey, 57, 135
Standard Stations, Inc., 22
State, Dept. of, 41
Steel, generally, 9, 65, 89, 153, 158-160
    drums, 65
    stainless, 62, 153, 159
    see also bolts, nuts, and rivets; conduit; metal rain goods; scrap; tin plate; iron ore
Stock ownership in other companies, 35, 64, 128, 131
Stocking, George, 25, 97, 109
Street lighting equipment, 60, 141
Substitutes, 30, 35, 42, 76, 95-97, 120
Sugar, 34-35
Supplying facilities below cost, 67, 166—see also leasing below cost, sale below cost
Surgical equipment, 66, 166
Swift and Co., 150
Switches, 140
Synthetic fibers, 33—see also orlon, nylon

Taft, Robert, 24
Technicolor, 151
Telephone, 99
Telephone equipment, 63, 141
Temporary National Economic Committee, 32, 46-47, 78, 90
Texas Co., 66, 135, 136, 137, 157, 158
Tin cans, 33, 36, 159
Tin plate, 65, 159
Tires, 33, 61, 66, 97, 137, 145, 147, 158, 161
Titanium, 60, 143

Tobacco, 62, 66, 153, 167—see also cigarettes
Tracerlab, Inc., 99
Trade-marks, joint, 129, 131
Tungsten carbide (hard metal alloys), 60, 84, 139
Turbine generators, 66, 163
Twentieth Century Fund, 25, 109-110
Tying contracts, 137, 151
Typewriters, 33

Union Carbide & Carbon Corp., 144
United Aircraft Corp., 125
United Fruit Co., 155
United Shoe Machinery Co., 22
U. S. Rubber Co., 66, 147, 148, 161, 163, 164
U. S. Steel Corp., 48-49, 63, 65-66, 80, 93, 158, 159, 160
Upholstery, 94

Vanadium, 144
Vertical integration, 11, 21-22, 37, 43-44, 108, 112-113, 120, 123, 132
Vested interests, 2, 11, 73, 98

Watkins, Myron W., 25, 109
Western Electric Co., 141
Westinghouse Electric Corp., 60, 66, 138, 139, 140, 163
Wheeling Steel Corp., 49
Women's garments, 109
Wool, 95
Woolworth Co., F. W., 63, 67

Youngstown Sheet and Tube Co., 49, 63, 65, 159, 163

Zaibatsu, 41-42, 106, 111
Zone pricing, 164, 168

Typography by
Jackson Typesetting Company

Printed by
Cushing-Malloy, Inc.